AN ACCIDENTAL
THEODICY

AN ACCIDENTAL **THEODICY**

Genuflexions on a Fractured Knee

Arvind Sharma

Published by State University of New York Press, Albany

© 2019 State University of New York

All rights reserved

No part of this book may be used or reproduced in any manner whatsoever without written permission. No part of this book may be stored in a retrieval system or transmitted in any form or by any means including electronic, electrostatic, magnetic tape, mechanical, photocopying, recording, or otherwise without the prior permission in writing of the publisher.

For information, contact State University of New York Press, Albany, NY
www.sunypress.edu

Library of Congress Cataloging-in-Publication Data

Names: Sharma, Arvind, author.
Title: An accidental theodicy : genuflexions on a fractured knee / Arvind Sharma.
Description: Albany, NY : State University of New York, [2019] | Includes bibliographical references and index.
Identifiers: LCCN 2017032622 | ISBN 9781438470078 (hardcover) | ISBN 9781438470085 (pbk.) | ISBN   9781438470092 (ebook)
Subjects: LCSH: Sharma, Arvind. | Hindus—Biography. | Knee—Wounds and injuries. | Theodicy.
Classification: LCC BL1175.S4235 A323 2020 | DDC 294.5092 [B]—dc23
LC record available at https://lccn.loc.gov/2017032622

10 9 8 7 6 5 4 3 2 1

For every bad thing there might be a worse; and when one breaks his leg let him be thankful that it was not his neck.

—Bishop Hall

CONTENTS

Preface / ix

Part I
The Accident / 1

Part II
The Aftermath: The Search for Meaning / 39

Notes / 117

Bibliography / 135

PREFACE

I broke my leg in an automobile accident in the summer of 1990 while teaching in the Faculty of Religious Studies at McGill University, Montreal.

I had always been interested in issues of theodicy. The accident gave it an existential edge and a personal focus it had hitherto lacked. This book is an account of the accident and its theodicean aftermath.

The events described in part I, which contains an account of the accident and recovery therefrom, are real. The personal names are fictional. In part II nothing is fictional, unless everything is.

Arvind Sharma

PART I
THE ACCIDENT

I

The day: Friday, June 8, 1990. The time: 4:47 p.m. The place: just outside the driveway to 3520 University Street (otherwise known as the Birks Building) at the outer perimeter of McGill University, Montreal. As I approached the driveway on the pedestrian walk I saw the light at the crossing ahead turn red. This meant, I thought, that I could safely cross the road, since University Street was a one-way street. I was wrong. I had hardly moved a few steps from the curb when I heard a bang. It came from my knee striking the side of a car, bang on. The next thing I knew I had fallen on my derrière, perilously close to a parked car but not on it. And right in front of me, now barring my vision, a blue car had come to a stop.

Before I knew what was happening a young woman rushed to my side from the sidewalk. She put her hand across my back as she bent down and shouted, "Don't move. Don't move." Then she asked, "Are you all right?" I looked around at everything from the car-handle level and said faintly, "I think so." Again admonishing me not to move, she shouted to a passerby, "Please call an ambulance. A person has been hit by a car."

In retrospect it is not hard to reconstruct how this fate had befallen me. As I had veered off the sidewalk, somewhat impulsively, to cut across the road on the hypotenuse of the Pythagorean triangle, a car that I had a moment ago passed on foot had begun to pull out of the parking spot. I hadn't looked both ways before crossing—right, left, right—as one is supposed to. I had just looked forward, in keeping with my "forward-looking disposition," as my colleagues would gently chide me later. Somehow the driver of the car also failed to spot me in the rear mirror. It was not as if an irresistible force had met an immovable object (when that happens a child is said to be born)—rather, a sluggish car had backed into an ambling pedestrian. But the doorknob of the car had hit the pedestrian in the knee and he now sat on his bottom, hors de combat in the Montreal rush-hour traffic in summer, during a month in which the rate of automobile accidents in the city goes up by over 10 percent. The accident, one would think, had a probabilistic point to prove, and I had become a statistic in this world of statistical contingencies. Not everyone can be a statistician, but anyone can become a statistic.

Not quite. To my considerable amazement the ambulance arrived in three minutes. But time passed slowly, slowly enough for me to learn that the young woman who stood solicitous guard over me was a student of nursing (or was it social welfare?) in the building next to Birks and close to the university gate, the very building in which I was to teach my Hindi class at 5:00 p.m. I even saw a student, Roger I think was his name, pass by, and we even waved to each other, under conditions that left me mildly embarrassed but left him totally nonplussed ("Is he going to hold the class in the middle of the street?"). I asked the young woman to call our departmental receptionist. After all, I had been felled virtually in front of the very building in which I professed. That I should call for her was not without its touch of irony. A few weeks earlier she had been knocked down by a motorcycle, carried to the hospital in an ambulance, and then released after a medical checkup. When this was narrated to me I looked her over and said, "Couldn't help giving a knock-out performance, could you?" She had fixed me with a withering stare. There was thus an irony in the situation. Nor was it a fortunate irony either. One should watch one's words, one may have to swallow them, sometimes in unexpected ways. I would not recommend this diet to anyone. So I wasn't surprised when she came down, put her hand behind my back, and after making sure

I was not gravely hurt, proceeded to inflict grievous bodily harm on my already wounded ego by saying, "You can't help making a scene, can you?," smiling ever so gently. This she said as she left, after I had told her to announce to the Hindi class that it would not meet today. And to think that I was going to give them a quiz today! Now the quiz was on me. After she had left, someone from the knot of people who had gathered at the scene asked me to try to stand. At first the red light of medical caution flashed through my mind, but it soon turned to amber out of my own curiosity. I tried to stand, but I could feel my knee wobble and then almost buckle. So I just sat down and started surveying the scene of my own accident with a rather strange sense of detachment. This, I presume, has something to do with the body's psychological defense mechanism called dissociation.

In the meantime, the driver of the car that had felled me had stepped out. The young woman attending me and now standing by my side had the good sense to ask him how he felt: "Are you all right?" "Yes, but nervous," he said, nervously. I felt like shaking his hand, but some strange sense of legal caution prevented me from doing so, lest it might be held against me in some unforeseen way. I now reproach myself occasionally, and sometimes even bitterly, for not doing so. Even if I cannot say whether I believe in it or not, at least I had been culturally gifted with the doctrine that others are only the instruments of our own karmic destiny.[1] But I did not use my gift. I did not shake his hand, which would only have been the Hindu thing to do. This ethical insight was clouded by legal fear, even though I knew not merely that accidents are virtually no-fault legally in Montreal, but that they are also no-fault morally in light of one's own karma. The Hindu sages would perhaps say that I had an "attitude problem." It inhibited me from employing the alchemy of goodwill in distress to convert my bad karma of the accident into the good karma of friendly forgiveness by merely giving my karma a fair shake. For by shaking his hand I would have been saying, in body language, "hard hit but no hard feelings."[2] But I hesitated lest the gesture be misunderstood—by him or others. I hesitated too long. The moment was lost.

I never saw him again.

By now the three minutes must have been over, as a man in uniform stood in front of me and had begun questioning me in French! At this the young woman by my side almost lost her temper and shouted at him, "He does not know French"; which was only the truth, alas only too true, even though I was living in the second-largest French-speaking city in the world. Before I could wonder whether this was also going to be fatally true for me and whether I was going to be a victim of the language war in Quebec in addition to being an accident victim, the man in uniform, after saying something to the young woman in French (I presume it was an appeal to stay calm), switched to English. After being asked whether I had lost consciousness ("no") or voided ("no"), I was put on a stretcher and swaddled in blankets as the ambulance headed for Hospital Royal Victoria up the hill, with the siren sounding. It had a very short distance to cover—the hospital was just up the road.

I did not even have time to thank the young woman for having been such a good Samaritan. Crisis and courtesy make strange bedfellows; sometimes they do not make bedfellows at all. Period. I could not even thank the young woman who had precipitated out of nowhere in my moment of dire need. She disappeared as mysteriously as she had appeared. It almost embitters one to think that life can be so thankless. All my subsequent efforts to locate her failed miserably, which was only to be expected as I had so little to go on. I did not know her name. She had said something about being enrolled in the building next to ours, but that led nowhere. Since that day the following Hindi couplet memorized in an Indian childhood took on new meaning: "Embrace every stranger, however shod; who knows who, among them, may be God."

It was soon after I was stretched out in the ambulance that the thought of *God* crossed my mind for the first time since the accident. "What!" I exclaimed to myself. "It took a good five minutes for me to think of God after I had only been rudely hit in the leg, when I teach religion all the time, and Mahatma Gandhi could take God's name in a flash while his chest was being pierced by an assassin's bullet." An accident sure separates the men from the boys, and I was among the boys. Almost two minutes later the thought of my motherland—India—crossed my mind. This was not an accident, it was a rude lesson in self-revelation! Although I have referred to India as my motherland, what I really mean by "India" is not so much India as a geographical area but as a zone of spirituality. In fact, Raja Rao somewhere defines India as a state of mind—a state of mind that sees things steadily and sees them whole, or what Kathleen Raine refers to as an archetypal seat of unique spiritual wisdom. I thus lay in the moving ambulance marveling at the discoveries I was making about myself—about what I thought I was, and what the sudden turn of events was doing to expose the gulf between who I thought I was and what I was turning out to be. This gulf, I had thought earlier, was nothing more than a chink that I would cover up by wedging in a small sliver of self-deception. It had turned out to be a gaping chasm over which one might still build bridges of fantasy, lowered over that moat by the pulleys of wishful thinking, but on which one could not dare set foot, however chivalrous one might feel. It has truly been said that we are not one but three persons: the person *we* think we are, the person *others* think we are, and the person we *really* are. For a rare and brief moment all the members of this trinity stood staring at each other in front of me.

The ambulance came to a halt and I soon found myself being wheeled into the emergency room. After some wait I was processed on the strength of my healthcare card, and then I had to wait for a doctor. The wait was long, or at least seemed so. I felt faint at times. On one occasion I dragged myself to the faucet for a drink; on another the husband of a woman waiting for a doctor behind a partition got one for me. I soon learned that one of course one repairs to a hospital after losing health, but one also soon loses one's privacy, or bits of it at least, although everyone is very nice and discreet. But such is the nature of the beast.

Time lay heavy as lead, both before and after the X-ray. The human mind is an interesting mechanism—it is capable of objectively identifying virtually all the possible outcomes of an adverse situation and yet subjectively attaches itself to the hope that the least painful one might eventuate. As I sat there, whiling away the hours, I feared that I might have a fracture but hoped the X-ray would turn out to be all right and they would let me go home the way Ann—the receptionist, remember, the one who was knocked out—was let go. I clung to the hope and began to worry about my future. I needn't have. It arrived soon enough in the form of the doctor who walked in, almost flaunting the X-ray, and announced, "You have a fracture," and proceeded to show me how my tibia had splintered just below the knee. "Perhaps it can be fixed with a cast," he mused. "Can you come tomorrow?"

"I live alone and will have to climb up four flights of stairs to reach my room."

"We had better find you a bed here then," he said genially, and disappeared for the night.

In due course one of the nurses wrapped up my leg with a coiling band to keep it firm, while the staff debated where to put me in the hospital. The issue was resolved quickly. I was assigned a bed overlooking the city lights. The view was rather beautiful but seemed so only for a fleeting moment. Physical pain had generated a kind of aesthetic irrelevance and imparted to the situation rather an anesthetic imminence that at the moment only sleep seemed capable of providing. I soon sank into fitful sleep with most of my regular clothes on. Among my last thoughts was this: "I get a bed in a hospital in Canada by just flashing a card!" If only we could have a system like this in India, and this time I meant the India of geography and not of some map of consciousness. It was with such patriotic, if somewhat pharoanic, fantasies that I soon lulled myself into sleep.

II

My first memory of the morning after (do they still respect me as a patient?) is that of an orderly carrying the breakfast tray high on his hand, heralding the advent of the day. He was black, and as I would probably qualify as a "brown sahib" I felt a certain sense of chromatic brotherhood. The bed to my left was unoccupied but the one right in front was occupied, and the bed to its left was also empty. By simple mathematics this meant that only two of the four beds were occupied. I feel I can state this with some certitude despite Einstein's warning that to say something in mathematical terms means that it isn't true. I presume he was speaking of higher mathematics.

We, the two occupants of the room, began by assessing each other visually and furtively at first, as we had our breakfast of oatmeal, boiled eggs, and tea or coffee. My roommate was short and slim, one might even say slight of stature, but had a sense of agility about him, which sometimes expressed itself in his darting hither and thither with a certain impish air—as when he would come to get my cream, which I did not consume, and which he liked but was strictly not supposed to have. It was forbidden to him because he was being treated for diabetes. This restriction he circumvented with my active connivance. He was a francophone who had travelled widely and in fact was visiting from Brittany, if memory serves. I am happy to say that he, like me, was single—a fact that immediately marks people out in my imagination on account of its singularity, not untouched by a smidgen of fellow-feeling. It also meant that he, like me, had no family visitors, though in my case this fact was soon to be modified by the arrival of my sister.

Literary if not poetic justice demands that I must now describe how I must have appeared to him, however speculative the description might be, with the dice loaded in my own favor by the fact that the "narratee" is identical with the narrator. He must have seen a tall dark man sprawled listlessly, and perhaps even comically, on the bed, his right leg in thermal underwear and his left in an extensive bandage, as it lay exposed through the slit in the long johns, attached to formal attire above the waist, its formal nature incongruously accentuated by the absence of the tie! The face had a faded and lost look about it, the hair disheveled and streaked with white. The whole scene must have suggested a certain lethargy not entirely distinguishable from an air of world-weariness, for the person seemed so laid back as to be virtually comatose.

Perhaps by a right that accrued to him as the senior resident of the room, my companion was the first to break the silence. Patients observe their own protocol unless a supercilious omertà or code of silence prevents them from speaking to each other. The language barrier was overcome by the fact that his knowledge of English was better than my knowledge of French (which is nonexistent except for one line, which I cannot repeat for fear of besmirching my reputation). The divide was overcome by raising monosyllabic expressions, or at best staccato phrases, to the level of articulate conversation.

"Accident?"
"Yes."
"When?"
"Last evening."
"Where?"
"Nearby."

And so it went. The linguistic barrier was not overcome in a giant leap, it was battered down by a persistent barrage of monosyllabic blows. I noticed, though, that as soon as our marital status was established to our mutual satisfaction—namely, that neither of us had one—we communicated more freely and cheerfully even within our linguistic confines.

III

Suddenly some people entered the room, provoking an eddy of activity. The group went toward the other patient, who was examined with curtains drawn. He had apparently been operated on, and the doctors seemed to be tidying things up—"scissor," "suture," "bandage," "looks okay"—and out they came. They exchanged a few remarks among themselves and with the patient and then disappeared as quickly as they had arrived, giving the room the atmosphere of an empty platform after the train has departed.

It was apparently time for morning rounds, for soon another doctor came in with a few interns in train. I recognized him as the man who had examined me the day before, a personable and pleasant person who informed me that he and his colleagues were not quite certain whether a cast would suffice or whether an operation was called for to set the bone. The decision would be made after a CAT scan. So in a short while I was wheeled in for tomography. By now the efficiency with which the place was run had begun to make an impression on me. It could be that I was impressionable—after all, I came from India, which, I think, was once described by Galbraith, then the American ambassador to that country, as an example of functioning anarchy; even Mahatma Gandhi wistfully aspired only to "ordered anarchy." This fact has been raised to the status of an approach to life itself in some Indian sayings, such as those that define a vehicle as anything that moves, that is to say, that can make do as such. But even by more objective standards, I venture to think, the place could be described as well run, at least so far.

During the day Ann arrived from the office, which was closer to the hospital than I had imagined. I suppose discomfort enhances distance and pain prolongs it even further. A familiar face was a sight for sore eyes. Ann moved briskly after spotting me, marching quickly to my side and planting herself firmly in the chair. "Here is your mail. Here is a note for you, here are your things, and how are you?" Ann had taken charge of the situation in her usual manner. She had gone over to the Hindi class and called it off for that evening. The timely arrival of the weekend meant that we had until Monday to figure out the shape of things to come. We decided that visitors would be discouraged from seeing me in my sorry plight, which, in effect, meant that Ann would screen them! I was learning more about palace intrigue now than I had from all my reading of world history and perhaps even Chinese history or even the history of Byzantium.

I think, however, that I have to thank Ann for making that one exception regarding the rule about "no visitors." It was perhaps around seven in the evening. The doctor had just come in and told me what I was beginning to fear—that the CAT scan had tilted the decision in favor of the operation. "What does it involve?" I had asked. "Oh," he said in a matter-of-fact way, "we will take some extra bone from your pelvis," he said this as he pointed to it, "and put it under the knee." And he pointed to the knee. All this sounded like a major operation to me, but the very casualness of his manner aborted any anxiety I might have had. While I was trying to come to terms with the fact that my body was about to be replaced with its own "spare" parts, he went on casually, "And it will hurt more up there," he said pointing in the general direction of the pelvis, "than down here." He was now pointing to my knee again.

He must have sensed that I was not a fully consenting adult and needed more information before he could have my "informed consent," for he decided to draw me a diagram of what they were going to do to me. However, between us, a professor and a doctor, we could not find a pen! So he went to the nurse's station to get one.

It was in this interlude that Natalie, whom I had vaguely known as one of the doctoral students in our faculty, appeared at the door. Her arrival was as total and complete a surprise as can be. One could call it a second accident—only that this one was more welcome, and any wreckage that was likely to result would consist of broken hearts. "Hi Natalie," I said but added hastily, "but the doctor is here."

"Does it mean that I should leave?" she asked, framed against the door, standing akimbo.

"Perhaps you could wait a while."

"All right," she said, and disappeared.

The doctor returned and showed me how I was going to be chopped up and then put together again. Natalie returned as he was explaining the finishing touches of my surgical destiny, which he had charted on a stray piece of paper (or was it a tissue?). I introduced them. He soon left, with instructions that I partake of nothing either liquid or solid after midnight. Only after he left did I realize that there was no need for Natalie to have been absent. What he had described may have seemed to be a somewhat esoteric procedure, but it was hardly private. Moreover, it turned out that it was not even esoteric—the nurses told me it was done all the time!

I was in a state of mild consternation when Natalie returned. I was afraid that the complication caused by her arrival at a time when the doctor was visiting me had meant that she had had to wait, and that this might have put her off. She had, years ago, been a student in one of my classes and was now a doctoral candidate in the faculty—and that was all I knew. I did remember her from the meeting of the graduate committee when her proposal was accepted, and also from the dinner we had with Professor John Hick when he was invited by our faculty as the annual Birks lecturer for 1989.

"I have Ann's permission to be here. She is not letting anybody else through," Natalie explained. So I was obviously well protected from any intrusion, howsoever well-intentioned.

Thereafter Natalie began to visit me in the hospital fairly regularly, albeit unpredictably. I was never sure when she would visit, but that she would come was reasonably certain. This was at a time when she had substantial personal issues of her own to deal with, such as the terminal illness of her mother. In other words, her concern for me seemed to be, as I suppose Christians would say, an act of pure grace. I throw in this last bit of autobiographical fact not because it is relevant but only to maintain the factual symmetry of the personal discourse in progress. Her intuitions of kindness were such that were I a believer in the supernatural realm, I would have had to consider her as yet another angelic precipitation from that realm. In fact when she appeared at a time when my vision was clouded by drugs, when my legs lay outstretched and tortured with pain, with much more of me visible than is normal, and with my eyelids leaden with exhaustion, she represented the incarnation of an aggregation of virtually every form of benign relief one could hope for, to such an extent that only the fact that she had been married and was not a nurse prevented me from hallucinating her as a visionary montage of the Virgin Mary and Florence Nightingale.

IV

Although the doctor had indicated that the afternoon was the appointed hour, the flurry of activity around my bedside that woke me up immediately suggested that something else was up, apart from me. Indeed, the time of my operation had been advanced to the morning; in fact it had been advanced even further, to right then, as in now. One is more used to postponement in surgical matters than preponement, but the alteration had been performed with such swiftness that I had no time to react, let alone reflect. All I remembered was signing some of my limbs away the previous night as I dosed off, with an intravenous drip in my arm to eliminate the trace of some infection detected in the pre-op test. The doctor who tested me was Lebanese, and the sentiment he shared with me as he left was that he was now going home to see his daughter. Being single myself, I keep overlooking the fact that most people around me have families. I see them by themselves and just assume that they live by themselves, like me. How self-centered can one get!

By now I was down in the operating area. It was like a fancy-dress ball, only everyone wore similar masks, which I perhaps did not fancy much. Soon I saw two eyes peering at me; the anesthesiologist wanted to know the relevant details of my medical history. "Have you had anesthesia before?" "Yes." "How did you feel?" "I love it." The anesthesiologist rolled her eyes heavenward in disbelief. Obviously she did not put much purchase on the obliteration of individuality and was oblivious to the Sufi sentiment that "my separate existence is itself a sin to which no sin I could commit can be compared." The question of whether I should be administered a total or spinal anesthetic never crossed the threshold of debate, despite my slight preference for the former. The anesthesiologist backed the other doctor, who also happened to be a woman, before I could say anything at all! It was a woman's world down there.

I do not recall having been numbed through a spinal before, but it was a relatively painless procedure. From the conversation among the doctors, I gathered that this is a common procedure in childbirth! We live and learn; the question now was, will I learn and live, for as they cut me open I heard a doctor say, "It is all bashed up, much worse than what the X-ray showed." Perhaps clinical detachment is infectious, all that sterilization notwithstanding, for that was the spirit in which I took the remark myself. At that moment they could as well have told me they were chopping the leg off.

Soon the operation was fully under way. The doctors expressed satisfaction that my condition was stable; there was a slight tendency toward arrhythmia but within normal limits. I can barely recall of the passage of time. Then I heard a doctor say, "This is a neat fit," and there were other self-congratulatory comments. The bottom line seemed to be that although when we opened him up he was in a condition far worse than we expected, now that we are closing him up we have done a far better job of putting him together than we thought possible.

But as I heard these comments I also sensed that the anesthetic was beginning to wear off, and I murmured my observation to the doctor. She said, "Okay, his block is coming off," and then she turned to me and said "We are almost finished. But I will give you something."

What did she give me?

It turned out to be really something. I quickly lost awareness of the body altogether and felt disembodied. I also started feeling vigorous rather than drowsy. I then repeated loudly and introspectively, "Who am I? Who am I? Who am I?" like a receding mantra. The next thing I found myself doing was chanting "OM." Then I proclaimed "God is great" and said "You doctors seem to be having a dandy time! I came here for a physical experience and am having a spiritual experience." That convulsed the doctors. They laughed so hard I thought *they* might need stitches.

As I said this I felt as if my body were being put in a sheet and rolled up like a mummy. I felt no pain or any other sensation. Just very light. Down in the postop room I opened my eyes, looked at the nurse, and exclaimed, "You look so beautiful!" She and all the attendants started to laugh. I had not realized that I was still under the influence of the drugs given to me on the operating table.

"What's so funny?" I asked crossly.

"Nothing. We are laughing with you, not at you," someone said.

I again closed my eyes with a smile.

When I opened them again the magic was gone! I was lying with all sorts of tubes hooked to me, all alone, in what now seemed like very drab and cold surroundings. Periodically a nurse would come and check my temperature and blood pressure. I started feeling the cold intensely and feared that it might set off an asthma attack. The nurse said she could not leave her station to get my inhaler from the tenth floor. From being someone full of spirit, I had turned into a drowsy forlorn patient in the twinkling of an eye. If I did not at the moment think that I was in one of the cold infernos of Dante, it was only because my mind lacked imagination and felt as listless as my body.

Someone asked me to wiggle my toe. I tried and said, "Sorry. I can't do it."

"You just did," the nurse said, to my astonishment. It was quite obvious that in the psychophysical organism that I was, my "psycho" was not quite in sync with my "physio."

Among the numerous people I had had to deal with since I was struck down, I could point to only two until now who showed any sign of insensitivity. One was a doctor and the other a nurse. The doctor was one of the team in the operation theater who insisted I just had to put up with the cold. I began to suspect that he was really asking me to put up with him. When I repeated the request to another doctor, the problem was taken care of right away. The nurse was the one in the postoperation room who seemed to wear a request-resistant armor and did nothing at all to help me get rid of the cold when I started feeling chilly. This time my luck changed only with the change of shift.

V

I had barely opened my eyes again with some sense of relief at being back in my own bed now, when I saw a young woman standing right in front of me with a measuring device in her hand.

"I am your physiotherapist," she announced.

"Okay. But I have just had an operation."

"I know," she said. "That's why I am here. You must do the exercises now!"

Surely her "now" is a figure of speech, I thought, or perhaps was linguistically operating as an enclitic with no reference to time or tense. But her next remark put an end to my escapist grammatical musings. "Right now," she said firmly. As she was apparently a francophone I permitted myself the reflection that English can be a cruel language.

"But I just had an operation," I protested again.

By now she had moved close to the bed and had placed her hand under my bandaged knee. I sat up to accommodate her prehensile intrusion.

"Good. Now bend," she commanded.

Amid a welter of moans and groans I did what I could. She applauded my efforts, just as they had been applauded after I had wiggled my toe.

I later learned the identity of this young woman. She was a francophone and her name was Madeleine. I viewed her arrival with mixed emotions, for the exercises she put me through filled me with apprehension. But as time passed, comprehension replaced apprehension as I began to understand what she was trying to do. The surgeon had done his job, it was now the physiotherapist's turn. But patients be warned: a physiotherapist can convert your hospital bed into a torture rack in no time. I was then asked to leave the bed and move on to the chair. To my further disbelief I was instructed to bend my leg at the knee as much as I could, within barely a day or two of the operation. I painfully tried to follow the instructions, and at one point the pain became so unbearable that I almost began to enjoy it, masochistically bending it to such an extent that I happily astonished the physiotherapist. The price of such exhibitionism was heavy, however: I passed out. In the next few moments after I came to, I kept trying to conceal that distressing moment of physical breakdown (with its appearance of cowardice), when in fact all it had done was to reveal the point of one's physical limitation, at a time when the illusions of one's quotidian confidence in one's physical powers had been shattered.

VI

It was now the third day after the operation and my temperature had not yet returned to normal. It would be normal but then shoot up again. Today it really shot up. The day itself had just entered that liminal zone when the nurses change shift—it was too late for the outgoing ones and too early for the incoming ones to worry about me. I was sweating, edgy, uptight, and no one seemed to care. It was particularly annoying that I could hear the laughter of the jocose company the nurses were keeping. One voice had a distinctly Indian accent. This added to my irritation, as I felt deprived of the attention I must have fancied I merited from a fellow Indian. Finally, my desperate and exasperated efforts got some attention and I demanded to see the doctor.

A woman soon arrived wearing a stethoscope with charming casualness. She identified herself as the intern in charge. She was the doctor whose benign interventions I was destined to acknowledge with a Christmas card. But today I was peevish. I said, with a touch of rancor in my voice, "If I am going to die at least let me have the satisfaction of knowing the disease I died from."

"Don't talk like that," she said, mercifully without taking umbrage. "What's the problem?"

"The doctor asked for tests to be done on me a long time ago to find out why I have postoperative fever and nobody has done anything. Moreover, I think I am running a very high fever."

Humor may make high temperature more bearable, but it does not reduce it. For the first few days the doctors were not too concerned that I ran a temperature or that it rose even higher toward evening. But it persisted beyond those few days, and in the evenings produced much discomfort. In the meantime I was downing gallons of water and orange juice to quench the insatiable thirst caused by my soaring temperature. I felt so physically agitated that I couldn't sit or even lie still.

One evening, Natalie arrived when I was in this condition and she soon asked to be excused, as if my discomfort, which she experienced virtually as her own, had caused her to resort to formal manners to give me the dignity of not being observed further in my distressing condition. It brings to mind a painful moment of my own when I had asked to be similarly excused from the presence of the late Professor B. K. Matilal, Spalding Professor of Eastern Religions and Ethics at Oxford University, whose company I would otherwise not merely keep but seek, when the visible pain of his affliction made me recall my formal manners and voluntarily withdraw from the philosophical discussions that had, until that moment, been in progress.

Natalie tells me that even in that condition I seemed more concerned that she not miss her flight, which was to take her to her gravely ill mother, than with my own plight—something that apparently raised me greatly in her moral esteem. I do not quite recall this, which only goes to show that in moments of delirious forgetfulness, one might be as capable of superior moral conduct as of inferior moral conduct.

By now the doctors were in a bit of a tizzy while I was sinking deeper into a state of self-absorbed worry. Almost a week had passed. All sorts of tests had been conducted, pronouncing me free of malaria and AIDS. After one particular meeting around me the doctor had even uttered that gentle understatement perfected by constant use: "We are concerned."

I remember the moment well. It was evening, and as the doctor left I could feel my psychic reserves ebb away. Since the accident, although I had experienced a wide range of emotions, despair was not one of them. Somehow my psychic reserves had held. But as they say in competitive sports, put enough pressure on the other fellow and the fellow will crack. I sensed that the point of "enough pressure" was now upon me. I had never quite, until then, taken stock of the situation. Things had happened so fast that it had seemed all would be over before I quite realized what had hit me. The realization now hit me that all might not be over in a nonchalantly somnambulistic way. I did my calculations: either things would get better or worse. If they got better, good; if they got worse, I would either end up incapacitated in some way, or dead. If I died there was no point in speculating any further than this: either one survived death or one didn't. Either way the issue is resolved. But as with life the real problem is not life but living; so with death the real problem is not death but dying.

I did not, however, venture too far with this line of thinking about what might happen. I focused, rather, on the fact that what might happen was not in anyone's control. The availability of religious ideas in Hinduism itself is virtually endless, and if you add to this the field of comparative religion, the supply increases further. With such vast resources to draw on, I nevertheless accepted the fundamental dualism of our experience of the universe, which testifies to the simultaneous existence of "spirit" and "matter," and I explored the two possibilities suggested by theism and naturalism. If there is a God, then everything is obviously in his hands now. And if there is no God and nature suffices by itself, then let nature take its course. Either way, although what lay ahead was unknown, there seemed little point in worrying about it. Having thus resigned myself to whatever lay ahead, I tried to get a good night's sleep. I remember saying to myself wryly, "At least get a good night's sleep before you die." Lest the reader be tempted to credit me with marvelous detachment, let me hasten to add that by now I was quite enervated and exhausted by the protracted conceptual struggles I had engaged in.

I suddenly felt a hand by my side. Then a voice in the dark said gently, "It is time to take your temperature." The minute ticked away, and the voice said, "It is normal." Just then another nurse entered the room quickly and said, "There is someone on the phone by the name of Natalie. She wants to know your temperature. Should we tell her?"

"Yes." I said, and rolled over, somewhat struck by the coincidence of the call. "Tell her," one nurse said to the other, "that the temperature is normal."

Only later was I to learn from Natalie that she had called on account of a locution. She knew more about the medical ambiguity of my situation than I did, and had fallen asleep rather worried about it. Suddenly she had been awakened by a voice out of nowhere, which commanded "Call the hospital." Obviously this disembodied voice preferred the imperative as the least verbose form of communication. Thus awakened, she had called the hospital at the very moment when my temperature was being taken in the wee hours of the morning and that also happened to be the time when it had turned normal. Do these things still happen in the fading years of our scientific twentieth century?

The doctors were quite relieved by this development. All tests had returned a negative verdict. The fever had disappeared as mysteriously as it had appeared. Like life. We don't know how it comes and how it goes. Like life, it had also produced some embarrassing moments, which in retrospect might even appear somewhat amusing.

VII

If nurses "sweat" and doctors "perspire," what do patients do—"expire"? Or do they too just sweat it out? I had just sweated it out. It was a quiet afternoon. Most of the other beds in my room were empty. The corridors were silent. God was in his heaven and the nurses were at their stations when Professors Singh and Dwivedi arrived, taking me completely by surprise. These were colleagues I knew personally who taught at other universities in Montreal and were part of the larger academic fraternity. I hadn't even known that they knew I was in the hospital. Professor Singh was a linguist from the University of Montreal with whom I had spent many afternoons in stimulating conversation. Professor Dwivedi was a statistician at Concordia University who organized aid to the Indians stranded in Kuwait after Hussein's invasion. He had also carried a consecrated brick for the building of the Rama temple at Ayodhya on behalf of the Hindu community of Montreal.

As they drew the chairs close I began to apologize to Professor Singh about a paper I had promised him but could no longer deliver in time, for painfully obvious reasons.

"We will not talk of those things," he said simply. "This is a social visit. We just came to find out how you were."

I told them all I knew and then added, "The injury is perhaps not that grave but the transformation in consciousness that is wrought by it . . ."

Professor Dwivedi and I exchanged a deep glance. Had he not said at a previous meeting that once a human being becomes convinced of his or her mortality, his or her life will never remain the same? The recent death of his own brother in India had awakened him to this realization, with the rather unexpected consequence that he had become more disposed to spend money freely, to the great annoyance of his wife! I too had just had my own intimation of mortality.

Professor Singh was pleased that the medical prognosis was not worse than it was, and it was doubtless a rational observation to steady the psyche, but Professor Dwivedi offered a more profound emotional comment before they left, which was soon because they were afraid of tiring me.

"Sharmaji, when Rama was exiled and Bharata returned to Ayodhya, Dashratha was in bad shape and soon expired, mourning the exile of his beloved son. Bharata too was heartbroken. Tulsidas says that at that time, when Bharata was disconsolate, Vasistha, the family preceptor, said to him, breaking into sobs, 'O! Bharata, listen! Destiny cannot be denied. Loss and gain, life and death, fame and infamy are in the hands of destiny.' "[3]

Then he turned to Professor Singh and said, "Let us leave now and let Sharmaji rest." Having said this, they departed, leaving me to contemplate the beautiful couplet he had recited, which is still enshrined in my memory.

His departure initiated a train of thought: If life and death are predestined, then are accidents too? Or does destiny neglect such minutiae? Does it proofread its decree, and then are they still accidents, or is it satisfied with its general tenor? Considering the possibility that everything could be predetermined in excruciating detail produced a psychological effect the very opposite of what I had expected. It calmed rather than agitated my mind, and the more seriously and minutely I entertained the possibility, the more serene my mind began to feel! If both Greek and Hindu religions possess the same fatalism, then the stoic character found among the followers of both these religions, who subscribed to what in my own more vigorous mental moments I would have considered a most preposterous doctrine, became explicable. However, these were not my vigorous mental moments, and as terror yielded to stupor I wondered if all the events of our lives were not just like scenes from a movie, already present there in the spool, present in infinitesimally minute detail, waiting to be played out in the theater of this world. All the world's not only a stage, it's a movie theater; all life is not just a play but something even more flimsy (I almost said filmsy): only a movie!

When I emerged from the state into which I had sunk, I returned armed with another realization, although it took me some time to recognize it. It was the realization that so far in the accident and its treatment, I had not felt the need to be part of a family. I had often wondered, as I led my single life, whether an accident or illness that was temporarily disabling would make me regret, or at least cause me to reappraise, my decision to remain single. Nothing of this kind had happened. Perhaps because the two colleagues who had visited me were married, my subconscious must have done some reckoning, for my thoughts were of this unheralded if not unexpected nature. The fact that I arrived at this conclusion could well be a tribute to the management of the hospital, but I think its roots lay deeper in the psyche and again in some kind of fatalism. I have softened the statement, for I seemed to believe that the presence or absence of a family can only make a marginal difference in such situations. For instance, a senior colleague, who was married, had passed away from a heart attack in a railway lavatory in India, and a wife had perished on the operating table while her husband waited in the lounge. Had the fact that they had been married made any difference? Could it have made any difference? Has the belief that alone we enter the world and alone we leave it become so deeply inscribed on the tablet of one's heart? I do not mean to imply, like Ambrose, that the "first man, if left to himself, would not have fallen," but that a person is ultimately left to himself or herself, fallen or not. To recognize that we are alone is not to be a loner but to dispense with the false cobweb of reassurance that our existence as a social animal might provide, and screen from us the true nature of our existence in the cosmos. As the popular Sanskrit saying reminds us: relatives turn away (at death) and dharma alone accompanies one thereafter. But perhaps the true test would come when I left the hospital. I had already had an anxious moment or two about it.

Some say that one's own suffering enhances sensitivity to the sufferings of others. In my case my suffering was making it more difficult for me to be more sensitive in this way. Professor Sivaraman, my colleague at Concordia University, had recently been diagnosed as suffering from a benign brain tumor. He occupied the only chair of Hindu studies in North America, and only a few months prior to this diagnosis we had traveled to Saskatoon to deliver talks to the Hindu community there, to which both of us had been invited through the courtesy of Professor Braj Sinha of the University of Saskatchewan in Saskatoon. Our return flight was one long philosophical discussion, which we had promised to continue. When I had recovered sufficiently from my own setback, I was finally able to call him. Our conversation was despairingly brief. His radiotherapy had depleted his reserves of strength and his last words to me were among the most poignant I have heard: "Pray for me." The haste with which he put the receiver down after saying that was an agonizing indication of how much effort even that brief conversation had been for him. I stomped my foot (the uninjured one) in indignation and cursed my own condition, which had kept me from talking to him earlier. One's suffering helps one relate to another's better? My foot! (No pun intended). Life only thrusts a knife in your stomach, and it knows how to twist it as well! A thorn in your foot does not necessarily make you more sensitive to the one in the foot of the fellow traveler—if it has gone deep enough into your foot, it can even make you forget that your fellow traveler, too, has a thorn in the foot.

VIII

Once my temperature was down to normal the sense of crisis passed. The surgeon looked approvingly at the change in the color of the cut at the site of my operation. To my untrained eye it looked the same, but his trained eye saw a different hue. It was only then that the full range of the fear my recalcitrant fever had generated became evident. Its continuance meant that I may have sustained an injury that had gone undetected and that might have become infected, with consequences difficult to identify but alarming to speculate about.

The word *amputation* was never mentioned, but did that possibility cross the mind of the medical profession? I do not know and perhaps don't want to.

In the meantime, the physiotherapist had been getting even bolder in the demands she made on me. A brace had been ordered for my leg, which did duty for the traditional cast. I was not to remove it, except for the physiotherapy sessions, during which I was now called on to learn to use crutches. These were the only items I actually paid for during my entire stay at the hospital, incredible as it sounds. I now realize why the Canadian Health Service is the object of such envy all over the world.

I began to learn to use the crutches slowly, perhaps too slowly, for Madeleine had to remind me at least once that I was a professor to speed up my learning process. Little did she know that professors don't learn, they only teach. The students learn! Besides, knowledge is not taught, it is "caught." She discovered this every time she had to catch me in her arms to keep me from falling.

As soon as I could move around and exercise on my own she began to spread out her visits. I used to exercise twice, during the morning and in the afternoon. I did this in the hallway and then on the steps, the difficult part. It usually took me close to twenty minutes to go through my routine. These details acquire meaning in the context of what transpired one afternoon. When I went out through the hallway to exercise, everything was normal, and when I came back it was again normal—but this time eerily normal, because there was a faint intimation of a lonely melancholy; only a few members of the normal staff seemed to be around. It was only later I learned that in the short time I had been away, a life had been lost! A nurse, who had had a liver transplant, had just returned from a six-month vacation and had collapsed right where I stood on my crutches as I was being told about it. The hallway was crammed with equipment, doctors, and nurses, and every effort to save him had failed. The hospital staff knew him because he worked there; his wife worked there too, and everyone was heartbroken.

I felt like a Buddha wanting to renounce and walk out of the world right then, but I hadn't quite learned to use the crutches yet.

By the time I did, the moment had passed. Moreover, although the incident had proved the Hindu saying right once again—"Life quivers like a drop of dew / Upon a blade of grass," I aspired, despite the fact that I was in a hospital, to fulfill the duties of my station in life, as the favorite Hindu text, the *Bhagavadgita*, exhorted me to in my favored interpretation of it.

The only problem was that I had no clear idea of my undertaking and was perhaps destined to pass into the hands of the undertaker while still in a state of confusion about my undertaking. Someone had defined Hinduism as a state of mind; it can often be a very confused state of mind.

IX

One of my research assistants was Stephanie, part Indian, part British, who dropped by when my friends Heather and Harry were visiting. She approached me where I was lying, drew up a chair, and exclaimed, "This is how I had seen you in my dream!"

Heather perked up. "My! My! What is all this dream stuff about?"

And then it came back in a flash. Some weeks prior to the accident, Stephanie had one day entered my office and asked, "Are you all right?"

"What do you mean am I all right? Never felt better," I had said, taken somewhat aback both by the personal nature of the question and the forthright manner in which she asked it. Stephanie is a pleasant, well-disposed person, but always correct and proper in her manner. A later episode illustrated her sense of rectitude. One day the chair I was sitting on in the room simply collapsed, and in breaking my fall with my outstretched arm I hurt my palm. It even drew some blood. The injury was so apparent that everyone I met would inquire about it. When Natalie asked me about it I began by telling her how I was sitting on the chair *alone* (I emphasized that) when it collapsed, and Natalie laughed so hard I thought her own chair might collapse. When I gave the same reply to Stephanie, she said, with a straight face, "I don't know what you are talking about" and cut me off. Obviously she has a very strong sense of observing proper form (how very British)! This made her question all the more surprising. I asked her what had prompted the inquiry anyway.

"It's just that I had this dream the other night. That you were in bed looking rather shriveled up, as if you had been ill or something. So you are all right?"

"I'm fine," I had said. I had in fact just returned from my maiden visit to the University of California at Santa Barbara, where I had delivered a talk while enjoying the hospitality offered by Professor Ninian Smart and his wife Libushka. I indeed felt that I was in fine fettle, which had made my reaction to Stephanie's innocuous question even more animated than it needed to have been.

Did Stephanie have a precognitive dream?

Maybe, but I had now to face the nightmare of leaving the hospital. A broken leg, on crutches, with no support system—where was I to go?

It was at such a moment that my sister came into the picture.

X

I like to think of myself as a person who is very fond of his sisters. I imagine the sentiment is universal, but it does not make it any less true. This of course could be sheer prejudice on my part but it is a prejudice I cherish, and if my alleged fondness for my sisters is nothing more than fraternal conceit, it is a conceit dear to me, based as it is on several years of cultivation. It applies even more to my youngest sister, since I have had more time to cultivate it in relation to her. We lived together under the same roof in the formative years of our lives, when my elder sisters were setting up their households.

Like me, my youngest sister, Shakti, abandoned domestic life for the academic. This fact also bonded us, I suppose. Paradoxically, however, although I am keen on my sisters I avoid my family and, as possible conduits of family influence, I also have had to keep my distance from my sisters to a far greater extent than I like. This distance has, however, been occasionally bridged by Shakti.

One day, about two months before the accident, I found a message on my answering machine announcing that Shakti was in town and indicating a number at which she could be reached. I prevaricated. Soon there was another message, which turned the tables of my recorded message to my callers on me. My message to them said, "Your mission, should you choose to accept it, is to leave your name and number." My sister's second message said, "I have accomplished my mission. Will you accomplish yours?" Finally, I did. I think my sister is one of those persons in my life who can make me act for purely sentimental reasons.

On meeting her I discovered that she was on a sabbatical and was spending it in Montreal: "I didn't let you know in advance because I knew that you would do all you can to prevent this from happening." So when the accident occurred and she offered to take me in for a week to smooth the transition to my own room, her presence here seemed Calvinistically predestined, even to a Hindu! She was fabulous. As she had herself single-handedly raised a family and also suffered from a fractured leg as a result of an accident on a mountaineering expedition, she knew about both the kind of suffering I was undergoing and the kind of care I needed. As I lay sprawled on the sofa, which doubled as a bed at night, I caught up with the story of her life with all its sensational details, as she did all the talking; I uttered short monosyllables or asked probing questions at proper intervals to keep the narrative flowing.

The most important single fact to emerge from her account was that she had been a follower of Sai Baba for several years now. I have a typical Indian interest in the so-called God-men of India, combined with perhaps an atypical reluctance to actually acknowledge any as a personal master. My sister, however, had crossed that threshold long ago and narrated in wondrous detail the working of the grace of Sai Baba. I attended the service at the Sai Baba center here in Montreal perhaps four times and soaked in the pious atmosphere that prevailed at these meetings. Often the disciples displayed the objects Sai Baba had materialized in their presence and presented to them. Shakti played the *bhajans* of Sai Baba and gave numerous accounts of his benevolent intervention in her life, including one in which he saved her from a possible rapist. It could be that in saying this I am being unfair to her, but it seemed at times that she wanted to draw me into the circle of his devotees as well. I, however, have now for so long been a person who believes in a coterie of one—the worst kind, I believe, according to Shaw—that—much as I admired the work Sai Baba was doing, my sister's devotion to him, and the powers he seemed to possess, ranging from the spiritual to the thaumaturgical[4]—I still felt that I had to follow my own path even though I wasn't sure what it was.

Her devotion, however, permeated her apartment and also kept me in a rather sublime mood. Her place was close to Natalie's, which meant that Natalie could also visit me, as well as her, at her convenience. In fact, for a while the two were thick as thieves!

The week went by quickly. By this time I had adjusted to the change. Ann had warned me that returning home to be on one's own, after being cared for in every way at a hospital, could be a disorienting, even depressing experience. I have to thank Shakti for the fact that it was only mildly so for me.

XI

To be entirely on my own in the theological college on crutches was a trying experience. It tried me in several ways. It tried my strength. It tried my patience. It tried my mobility. And when there was a fire in the neighboring Presbyterian college and we had to evacuate, it tried my composure. It was also a humbling experience, but fortunately never a humiliating one. In fact I was helped by so many in such unexpected ways at the college that after I recovered I felt the need to have a notice posted in the college acknowledging my indebtedness to all the residents.

But it was a long time before the notice came to be posted, as my recovery was slow. The doctor, within a week or two of the operation, had taken one look at the X-ray and placed me immediately in intensive physiotherapy.

My trips to the physiotherapy unit were an ordeal I underwent twice a week, loyally accompanied by Natalie. After my workout, I needed almost half an hour to recover. Then we would eat in the hospital cafeteria. That is how she discovered my weakness for tapioca pudding!

During this entire period Natalie stood steadfastly by me, so steadfastly that some members of the academic community were overheard to wonder if they also might not be better off with a broken leg! It was largely because of her "tender, loving care," as the cliché goes, which happened to be as true in this case as it is trite, that I was not overcome by a feeling of utter helplessness. When she could not make it, Stephanie would take over, and between them they saw me through those most difficult days—right from wheeling me down two blocks to the office to virtually spoon-feeding me as I lay incapacitated, and I realized that the expression "ideas have legs" is essentially metaphorical in significance.

One day Natalie stopped by on her way back from her class in Judaism, and I opened her book of Talmudic sayings. My eyes fell on the following statement of Hillel: Everything is preordained but freedom of will is given.

I was destined to meditate for long hours on this paradox without fathoming it.

I do not know whether it was predestined but for a month I tried my best, yet the knee would just not bend beyond a certain point. It was as if I was given the free will to try as I might and try what I might, but it was predestined that it would not bend beyond a certain point. This is indeed how Moshe Idel of the University of Jerusalem was to explain it as one possible way to understand Hillel's oracularly enigmatic statement. I kept dutifully doing all the exercises at home, and just as in the beginning Natalie had accompanied me for the hospital visits, now my sister took her place, until I was able to make it to the hospital on my own. In every way I was coming along fine, except that the flexibility still frustratingly eluded me.

Then one day, as I sat despondently in the chair to rest and recover after another failed attempt, it suddenly struck me: "So this is what the word *depression* means!" I had never really understood the meaning of that word until then! Now, it seemed, I not only understood its meaning, I perhaps had become a victim of it as well. And then Sandra called from Sydney, Australia. I had befriended

Sandra when I was teaching at the University of Sydney during my ten-year sojourn in Australia. I must have seemed really down and out, for from halfway around the world she said "A-R-V-I-N-D"— stretching out each syllable in matitudinal melodic resonance: "I have never seen you like this. You are always so cheerful." Then she had burst into tears.

Her emotional intervention was curiously therapeutic. The intensity of her affectionate sympathy worked like shock therapy. It not only prevented the downward emotional spiral from going into a tailspin, it arrested the downward movement itself. Although my physical condition was unchanged, my attitude toward it had changed in some indefinable way. Had depression, by some curious alchemy of affection, been resolved into hope or at least resignation? I do not know.

The phase of depression did not last long. The clouds lifted in less than a week. In fact they began to do so soon after Sandra's call. How different the landscape of Eden looks when that dark pterodactyl of depression descends with its sinister satanic swoop! I was also both touched and mystified by the role my brief conversation with Sandra had played in dispersing the gathering darkness with just a mere point of light, a glistening tear as it were. The reason for this is a rather curious one, I think, which I now relate at the risk of losing my readers. While living in Sydney, at that stage of our lives, we, like Dante, had found ourselves in the middle of a dense forest. At that time we tried to regain a sense of direction with the help of the mystical path, the map of which is said to be coded into the very genes of the Hindus. I had barely travelled the path myself. Let us just say I had a general sense of the direction in which the clearing might lie. Soon thereafter two incidents occurred that suggested that I may have pointed Sandra down the mystical path (for want of a better word), but she had already traveled further along it than I, and far enough for me to take some pointers from her. I may have been the cartographer, but she had turned out to be the wayfarer. Two incidents testified to this.

The first incident occurred when I was sitting in my office at Sydney University one day and Sandra stopped by. As I saw her enter the room I said, "Want to listen to some Hindu mumbo jumbo which I am reading?"[5]

"Let's hear it."

I was reading a rather abstruse discussion—in the form of a dialogue—between a swami and his disciple on one of the more recondite aspects of Hindu mysticism, and I just began reading aloud what I had been reading in silence. This came as a relief to me as I had trouble following the point. Suddenly, as I read out the problems posed by the disciple, she began to provide the answers, even before I came to them. I would pause to wonder how so intricate a question would be answered, and before I had read any further, an answer would come floating across the table, which would then uncannily match the answer given by the swami. And when I would express surprise at the coincidence, she would simply say, "But don't you see there can be no other answer?"[6] Well, I didn't until it was shown to me. This happened thrice in succession as the discourse became increasingly rebarbative for my taste. Finally I said, in happy frustration at this state of affairs in an affected stentorian tone, as I saw my spiritual leadership slipping out of my hands, "I am the Hindu here."

"Obviously I am the Guru then," she had retorted in the same spirit.

As we doubled up with laughter, I could not help wondering where she was coming from. What was all abracadabra to me seemed ABC to her!

The next incident occurred at her home, and on this I might lose the reader forever.

"Tell me about meditation," she said one day.

"I thought I had been invited for a cup of tea . . . English tea," I added, with a pause for effect in view of her British extraction. I was obviously trying to dodge the issue. But she was more determined than I had bargained for:

"This is my cup of tea."

While doing doctoral work at Cambridge I had supported myself through school by teaching meditation at an Adult Education Centre. I think they let me do it because I had the right color—the baked

Indian look of a defrocked peripatetic swami. Anyway, since Sandra insisted, I put her through the paces as it were, hoping to have some tea soon thereafter.

The meditation session is usually concluded by chanting OM in unison after the silent phase is over, so I chanted OM and waited for life to return to normal. It didn't. She did not chant in unison with me as is customary. I couldn't see her. She was seated at a distance from me and the curtains had been drawn to avoid distraction. In the meantime, evening had set in. I recited OM once again. Again there was no response. I waited for a while and chanted OM again. Still no response. In some of my sessions people had fallen asleep and I wondered if that fate had befallen her. A strangely secular vespertine reflection crossed my mind—perhaps we should have had tea first!

I just waited in the dark and was beginning to get worried when finally she stirred and said: "I had lost my voice! I tried to say OM each time but my vocal chords would not respond."

I was ready to go into shock. I may be an irreverent Hindu but I had picked up enough mystical lore to realize that there were supposedly three main stops on the path to inner knowledge. First you lose consciousness of the world; if you go in deeper you lose your voice (one explanation of the silence of the Yogis?); and if you delve still deeper you stop breathing. Body-heat is said to be the only remaining sign of life in the highest trance. Here I was expounding yoga, caught up in the intricacies of my own exposition for over a decade, and she had crossed over to stage two in her first sitting! This had never happened to me. I had lost my voice in the sense that I had gone into long silences not knowing what to say, but not like this. I might have begun holding her in superstitious awe but for the fact that we used to watch *Dallas* on television together when we could!

I wondered long on this uncanny ability of Sandra to penetrate to the core of matters spiritual—both intellectually and experientially. Was being "pure of heart" really the secret? For she was the only person to whom I would have applied that description, of all the people I knew at the time, including myself. Be that as it may, these experiences that I had with her seemed to impart to her words a very subtle and intangible power, almost mystical, to dispel despair. Not to respond to her outpouring of sympathy would have amounted to spiritual betrayal.

In any case, in the meantime, I had made considerable gains. I had resumed teaching the Hindi classes; to everyone's astonishment, not least my own, I was wheeled into the classroom by a bevy of young women, many of whom were students. Soon I was even walking on my own, and as a dare I even undertook a trip to Cambridge, Massachusetts. However, the knee still refused to flex fully and the Hindu tribute to God as someone who can make the lame walk seemed to remain the expression of a pious hope rather than paean to a miraculous deliverance.

By now it was time to see the surgeon again. When I went in for the second consultation with the doctor, along with Natalie, who kindly chose to accompany me despite the numerous claims on her time, the doctor dropped the bomb. The knee *was* stuck, just as I had feared. Then there was another explosion—only a slightly delayed one: another operation had to be performed, and as soon as possible. The cartilage had calcified and had to be chipped to restore flexibility, and soon. I had counted on a second operation being performed—if it came to that—in December, if it were to take place at all; but it had to be done now, in October. This was the second detonation of the same bomb, and the emotional shrapnel was worse.

XII

Once I had emotionally adjusted to the new timetable it was not so bad. Everything went fairly smoothly, and right on the table the doctor demonstrated the increased flexibility that had been achieved through the operation by swinging and swiveling my lower leg. To retain this gain, however, my foot was latched to a machine after the operation, which, for three days and nights consecutively and constantly, if gently, kept flexing the knee to the required extent.

Once again, within minutes of my operation, a physiotherapist appeared and asked me to perform! I couldn't believe it. She had a scale and wanted me to score "ten" in bending. Despite my morphine-enhanced state I howled with pain while falling abysmally short of ten. In the beginning our relationship was a bit frosty, but it soon thawed, and on the last day she was actually joking with me.

In the meantime the machine kept doing its work. I had gotten used to its operations the way one gets used to wearing glasses. After a while some appendages become parts of oneself, or at least extensions of oneself. Natalie had stopped by to provide some welcome company when all of a sudden Aziza, who had immigrated to Canada from Iran, turned up. She looked all torn up. She came right close to me and said: "Could I talk to you please?"

Natalie was about to leave anyway and Aziza's sudden arrival, and the difficult condition she seemed to be in, made Natalie leave us right away.

"Hanif has broken up with me," she said briefly.

Now that I have lived for over fifty years on this planet, romantic vicissitudes—whether one's own or those of others—have lost some of their impact. They tend to do so with the passage of time. Yet each such vicissitude also constitutes at least a time, if not a rite, of passage. Although one feels blasé about the fact, one is still sensitive to the impact—especially on one's friends.

I first met Aziza when she began to work as a waitress at a restaurant around the corner, where I am a regular. Although she was from Iran, she completely disowned the Ayatollah, to the point of criticizing my sister for endorsing his "sacred rage" against the West. After all "until Karl Marx and the rise of communism, the Prophet [Muhammad] had organized and launched the only serious challenge to Western civilization that it had faced in the whole course of its history. . . . the attack was direct, both military and ideological. And it was very powerful."[7] Although it had lost much of its power over the past two centuries, the Ayatollah at least reminded the West how powerful it had been or could be. The fall of communism and the rise of Islam should not obscure the fact that, despite difference in content, they share striking similarities in structure. Islam, like communism, insists on control of the state apparatus rather than that all citizens of such a state accept it. Islam, like communism, lives in the confident expectation of ultimately embracing the entire world. Islam, like communism, offers a unified and universal worldview, but a worldview that is historically immanentist in the case of communism. In the case of Islam, it is majestically transcendent, and thus, like communism, less open to collapse in the face of cognitive dissonance. Should Islam ever replace communism as the new threat to the Christian West, it will prove much more potent than communism. This fact made no impression on Aziza at all—it was not just the Ayatollah or Islam, religion per se had little to offer to dear Aziza.

I used to eat regularly at the eatery, and regularity bred familiarity. In the course of these virtually daily encounters, I familiarized her with Ann Faraday's concept of dream power. According to Ann Faraday our dreams disclose our *true* feelings about a certain situation in life, feelings that we may even be concealing from our conscious selves in the course of daily life. These feelings are revealed by our unconscious self through the medium of dreams. This interpretation of dreams by Faraday worked so well with Aziza that she was sold on it. After the breakup with Hanif she narrated a dream in detail to me and asked me to interpret it. I forget the details but remember the interpretation: "You want to have your children with Hanif." She had shrugged her shoulders.

I first met Hanif when I visited Aziza at a hospital between my two operations. She had come down with a renal infection, but by the time I saw her she was well on the road to recovery. We were conversing—as she tried to keep the drip out of the way—when Hanif arrived. He meditated. He was familiar with Eastern thought. When we dined together at Aziza's place, he even blamed the Arabs for forcing Islam down the throat of the Persians. If the conversion was forced, I wondered how the Persians could be such ardent followers of Islam, to the point of courting martyrdom. She was obviously very fond of him, inasmuch as outsiders can make judgments about matters so intimate that one wonders if the truth about them can be known to anyone except those concerned. And now he had left her.

"Why? What reason did he give for leaving?" I asked.

"He wanted his own space."

"I can relate to that." I said, laughing. "Anyone can."

She moved her head from side to side in disapproval, smiling all the time. "Mr. Arvind . . ." I liked her when she called me that, using my first name as my second and second as my first. "Mr. Arvind," she repeated, "How can you say such a thing at such a moment?"

"I just did!" I thought to myself. But caution was called for. So I said aloud, "What does he need his space for?"

"To pursue his spiritual . . ." she rolled her dark eyes heavenward, as she spoke, "To pursue his spiritual goals . . ."

"This is again something I could . . ."

I was not allowed to finish the sentence. She was sitting quite close to me now. She gave a reproachful shove to my shoulder. "Mr. Arvind, how can you say that . . . whose side are you on?"

"Why, yours," I said, "I hardly know him. But men do have spiritual longings women may find hard to understand. Of course women have spiritual longings which men may find hard to understand—like the king whose wife left him because she loved God more."

"He talked to you about karma over the dinner and you talk to me about it often. Is it good karma to suddenly dump someone like this?"

The delicacy of my situation was not lost on me. How was I to defend spirituality vis-à-vis morality? I couldn't. Or perhaps I could.

"It is easy to choose between good and bad—and for you he is bad. But it is more difficult to choose between relative good and relative good . . . For him you are not bad—he is going after something relatively better . . ."

"Yeah, like another girl," she scoffed.

"Is another girl involved?"

"No."

"Then why don't you accept his spiritual involvement."

"Then why did he get involved with me?" She demanded to know. Now how could I answer that? Besides, I was beginning to feel that I was getting on her off side. My attempts to explain Hanif's behavior as I understood it were being interpreted as an endorsement of it.

Aziza was heartbroken and mystified; I was mystified that the relationship should have ended as swiftly and abruptly as it did. There was no doubt in my mind that Aziza had great hopes from it. A broken knee and a broken relationship are hard to put together: they have no leg to stand on.

It seemed, however, that the time was nigh for me to at least try, for they told me that I could leave any day now. Finally the day of my final discharge arrived. It was on that last day, on the eve of my discharge, that I almost lost my nerve. I had to be discharged in someone's care once again, but no one had arrived. The machine had been removed, and when I tried to flex my knee I couldn't. Perhaps I was overanxious. Soon the doctor dropped by almost absent-mindedly. Obviously I looked as I felt. He remarked that I looked quite lost. I was. I had lost my nerve.

And then suddenly everything began to fall in place. The person in whose custody I was to be released, Asoka, finally turned up, with Natalie as a bonus. Then on our way out we ran into an Italian friend. In fact it was the enforced delay of her arrival that had compelled me to requisition Asoka's help. So finally I left the place in good and ample company.

When I went in to resume physiotherapy, the physiotherapist almost had an anxiety attack on discovering that I was hardly any better off now than before the operation. However, having lost my nerve already, I had nothing to lose. So I coolly told him, "Give me some time and let me try." Somehow I hit on one method out of the many recommended that began to work for me, and I gradually kept working at it, upping the ante as I progressed. Soon, to our mutual surprise, I began regaining my flexibility and gradually went past the old block. Within two weeks I was beginning to feel optimistic. Soon the physiotherapist told me to exercise at home and seek a final appointment with the doctor.

The appointment went smoothly. The intern checked me first and told me I was a lucky man to be in the condition I was in, after having had the kind of accident I had had. Another doctor came in, checked me out, said "Bon," and made the thumps-up sign. Then my own doctor came in and pronounced me okay. "Of course, the knee will be weaker and you are more likely to get arthritis having had the accident, but you can lead a normal life." A normal life? "What is the norm anyway?" I found myself asking, as I got up from the examination table and slipped into my pants.

XIII

The doctor had declared me fit; the realization that such indeed was the case came in a rather dramatic and unexpected way. I had once again made my way to Cambridge, Massachusetts, to confer with an eminent colleague, when I discovered that my mentor played the saxophone in a band. The surprise did not end there—the band was going to play the next day at the Harvard Divinity School. I thought music might soothe an accident-ravaged breast, and when I arrived another surprise was in store. It was music, but to the accompaniment of dance as well, if one wished! I was driven to this dance by Lisa, who had visited me a few times in Montreal, and whom I had met a few times in Cambridge. It was a lovely evening. Perhaps I got carried away, but as the saxophone struck a vibrant note I asked Lisa if she might take the floor with me—at the risk of having to cart me away physically if I collapsed.

We took the floor. The music was soft. We moved gently at first but then the music began to pick up pace and movement. So did we. We passed by my mentor and he smiled. We looked at his wife and she nodded. As the music rose to a crescendo and I was still on my feet, I realized that the accident had now indeed become an incident.

XIV

Toward those who had seen me through this crisis—from doctors and nurses to friends and colleagues—I felt immensely grateful, but I tried not to be fulsome in my acknowledgement of it.

It is a curious fact that although the word "ungrateful" is often heard, one hardly ever hears the word "overgrateful," doubtless partly because of the pious if naive belief that one cannot be thankful enough for favors one has received. But it seems that part of the morbidity of disease may not merely be physical but also ethical, in the sense that what others do professionally for us we take personally. It is of course a nice sentiment all around to feel grateful, but it can degenerate into a sentimentality that even the benefactor may find irksome. After all, none are more aware of the deficiency of language than the grateful, a fact I think we implicitly acknowledge when we say to our benefactors: "I cannot tell you how grateful I am."

Both God and gratitude are ineffable.

PART II

THE AFTERMATH: THE SEARCH FOR MEANING

I

The physical recovery from the accident was now nearly complete, although it was gradual. My first bold move had been to visit Cambridge across the border, even after the first operation. I was stiff-legged, but not about to be stiff-armed by adversity. Then came the second operation and another round of intensive physiotherapy. I again took to it religiously. The climax came when toward the end, a few days after my final appointment with the doctors, I went up for a final tryout, only to be told that my physiotherapist was not in. He had injured his own knee in a ski accident! I had to laugh. I doubt if it was genuine comedy, but it was genuine irony! The irony was, however, somewhat softened by the fact that he had sustained his injury while playfully skiing on the snows of Quebec, and not, like me, while crossing an ordinary street on an ordinary day. In any case, to signal my recovery I attended the annual meeting of the American Academy of Religion in November, sans crutches, sans stick, soon after the final operation. On returning, as I lay down on my bed in the room in the college, I suddenly burst into tears, to my utter surprise. I still don't quite know why. Is tiredness a form of sadness? I was actually smiling, and tears were rolling down my cheeks. I was reminded of the day when for the first time, as a child, I saw the amazing phenomenon of sunshine sweeping the scene and rain falling at the same time. Until then I had not considered the coexistence of rain and sunshine as an actual meteorological possibility; they had existed in my mind only as polar opposites that could only possibly come together in a poet's imagination.

When the accident occurred I wanted both to recover from it and to find out why it had happened to me. But I had to prioritize, and the first priority had to be recovery. Now that I had recovered, I wanted to know why it had occurred in the first place. It has been said that "faith takes care of the ultimate incongruities of life, while humor does nicely with the intermediate." What are they to do who respond to humor but not to faith? Must the ultimate incongruities of life remain unreconciled for them? Must one always be a fool, half the time in a comic and half the time in a tragic sense? But fool and wise alike must be healed.

The physical recovery, however, was quicker than my philosophical recovery, which was quicker than my theological recovery—which is still in progress—but I had no clear criteria to judge what was happening. It is even hard to tell whether one is progressing or regressing. So has there been any progress? It is too early to say, as the Chinese say when asked about the effects of the French Revolution. This is also how some Indian historians respond when called on to assess Gandhi's place in history. The wound had healed, but the hole the accident tore in the fabric of meaning remained to be mended. I sometimes wonder whether I am entitled to spank all the theodicies of the world on a wounded knee, and whether it is not immodest of me to apostrophize, "O God, did you have to break my leg to have a leg to stand on?" However, as I reflect on the issue further I am less assailed by self-doubt in raising the issue: why the accident? The reason for feeling this way may be as trivial as the conversational banality, "It is the principle of the thing!" Or it can be as profound as "Why does anything happen one way and not another, good or bad?" This approaches the existential depths of the Heideggerian question, why should there be something rather than nothing? If one finds the latter formulation more satisfying, one is perhaps entitled to congratulate oneself on being a well-educated person, but does it mean that one is any closer to the right answer? Or any closer to the right question, for that matter?

The question, however, not only arises but persists. Why? Were I still wallowing in self-pity I perhaps would have asked, why *me*? However, physical recovery had also provided a corresponding measure of psychological recovery, and I was happy to leave myself out of the question and just be a witness to it—perhaps only obtruding into the discussion now and then to point out a moral or adorn a tale with examples drawn from my own experience. I also tried to bypass as too formulaic the formal philosophy-of-religion approach to the question of theodicy in my quest for an answer, although some might think it is the obvious place to start. Some philosophical spadework, however, is indeed inescapable. One could categorize four reactions to the problem: its solution (still being attempted logically); its resolution (in terms of a higher theological context); its dissolution (by denying one segment of the problem theoretically, e.g., the reality of evil); or by focusing on practice instead of theory and responding psychologically to it as a challenge, instead of logically looking for an answer. One could distinguish between evil and suffering and between the problem of evil and the problem of suffering, Christ on the cross illustrating the dramatic divide possible here. One could also distinguish between moral order and moral justice. As the race riots in Los Angeles in May 1992 demonstrated, whites might worry about order and blacks about justice; law and order may perpetuate injustice, and the search for justice may rock law and order. However, these distinctions become important when we *think* about experience rather than being so in the actual experience, for it is as difficult to feel clearly as to think clearly, though perhaps both are necessary.

II

Were one harder of heart as well as head, one might ask, as someone does in the momentary clip of a foreign film that flicked across the TV screen the other day, *Why ask why?*[1] One must ask not merely out of curiosity, but rather much more so out of sensitivity. Philosophy, at least in the West, it is said, is born out of a sense of wonder; in the East, where religion and philosophy according to received wisdom are not sundered, the question is rooted not merely in curiosity but in sensitivity. When the Buddha plunged into the forest to solve the riddle of life, after encountering a sick, an old, and a dead person in turn—as tradition picturesquely depicts him doing—it was not because *he* was old, or sick, or dying. He was sensitive enough to introject the suffering of another into his own psyche to the point where the actual misery of someone else forced him to come to terms with the potential misery of his own, if we are going to be so uncharitable as to factor compassion out of his personal equation. The prick of a needle may be as effective as a Holocaust or a Hiroshima, when it comes to setting the psyche in motion in that direction. Let me slip this in before my continual cynicism begins to irritate—that the prick of a needle on one's own hand, as one maladroitly tries to sew one's own button right *here*, might cause one more pain, at least momentarily, than an atom bomb dropped out *there*.

It is, of course, quite possible that despite the accident I could have continued to indulge in the mysticism of the healthy-minded, à la William James. To one imbued with such mysticism, somehow the question of suffering does not pose a problem. Coming to grips with the question of suffering belongs to the mysticism of the sick soul. In Jamesian terminology, then, not only had my fracture made me sick in body, my raising the question of why it should have happened had made me a sick soul—in a healthy sort of way, though, for James thought that the mysticism of the second type involved a deeper penetration into the nature of reality than the first.

III

Actually, raising the question of "why?" possesses a theodicean element in itself—for it converts, or at least extends, a physical and/or emotional trauma into a moral or theological dilemma and thereby attenuates it, if it does not alleviate it. And as I raised the question, I began to play with several paradigms. It was like a child playing with a jigsaw puzzle—sometimes the pieces would come close to fitting, but one vital piece would be missing. And sometimes, when all the pieces seemed to fit, one's hand would shake and it would fall to pieces again. Or, even when the pieces seemed to fit and the hand was steady, someone passing would inadvertently knock it out of one's hand and the cosmos would again be reduced to chaos. Was the message that the pieces never fit, and trying to make them fit, going on with the attempt, was the name of the game? That as one's pain and earnestness diminished and the fun component of the exercise overtook them, one realized that this is what it was all about—all a play (*lila*) of some kind? The Advaitins—the nondualist thinkers of Hinduism—haven't quite figured out yet why the eternal immutable Brahman appears as this changing world. Is figuring it out what it is all about, like trying to see darkness with the help of a torch? But even though the torch helps us see *in* darkness, can it help us see darkness? Is this the *maya* of *maya*, the illusion of an illusion? However, is not *maya* more like double vision? After all, it is not *maya* that appears as the universe; it is *maya* that *makes* Brahman appear as the universe. Does it ever appear by itself? Is this how conclusiveness is dissolved in elusiveness, and the pursuit of happiness, in the end, is reduced to the happiness of pursuit?

IV

I was not about to give up yet. Why not keep God and godhead out of the picture at least for the time being, even if the polychromatic journal of the Hare Krishnas exhorts one to hark "Back to Godhead."

Gradually over the months, like oozing drops of water leaks forming a configuration on the seeping wall, a pattern seemed to emerge. One could distinguish three kinds of worldviews: a moral worldview, a rational worldview, and a natural worldview. As one moved from one to the other, the problem of suffering became less acute. According to a moral worldview, suffering would be caused by breaches of morality. What rule did I break, and when, to deserve what happened to me? The question can be very sharp, even poignant, especially as rarely, except in cases of "poetic justice," is an answer forthcoming. Poetic justice, however, does not always paraphrase into philosophical prose. According to a rational worldview, suffering could still have a cause, but the cause need no longer be moral. It can be physical, for instance, or just commonsensical: "When the city burns, does the temple escape?"[2] A moral worldview obliged me to seek the explanation of the fracture in some grievous bodily harm I may have caused, but if I espoused a rational worldview, the fact that the person who backed the car into me was an inept driver would suffice as an explanation, as would the fact that I acted impulsively in trying to dart across the road. In fact this could easily be converted into a no-fault explanation. I was lost in the blind spot of the rearview mirror—that was the cause, and neither of us were to be blamed. A natural worldview makes things even simpler. Accidents happen—why, they have been known to happen in the happiest of families, *pace* Dickens. And accidents happen with a certain regularity, even predictability. The anonymous statistical probability this time came up with my name![3]

The combinations of these theodicies produce exciting results. For instance, one could have a hyphenated rational-natural theodicy, where the word "rational" includes the irrational, thanks to the glories of the English language in which "a fat chance" and "a thin chance" can mean the same thing. Rabbi Kushner says, "To grab a gun and shoot at innocent people is irrational, unreasonable behaviour, but I can understand it. What I cannot understand is why Mrs. Smith should be walking on that street at that moment, while Mrs. Brown chooses to step into a shop on a whim and saves a life. Why should Mr. Jones happen to be crossing the street, presenting a perfect target to the mad marksman, while Mr. Green, who never has more than one coffee for breakfast, chooses to linger over a second cup that morning and is still indoors when the shooting starts?"[4] A hyphenated moral-rational theodicy can be equally provocative. The biblical narrative tells us that by the end of the sixth day God had finished the task of creating the world, and on the seventh day he rested. Did he rest too soon? May we suppose God didn't quite finish by closing time on the afternoon of the sixth day? We know today that the world took billions of years to take shape, not six days. The creation story in Genesis is a very important one and has much to say to us, but its six-day frame is not meant to be taken literally. Suppose that creation, the process of replacing chaos with order, were still going on. What would that mean?"[5] It would mean

THE AFTERMATH: THE SEARCH FOR MEANING / 45

that while "most of the time, the events of the universe follow firm natural laws . . . pockets of chaos remain."[6]

One might wonder whether such "pockets of chaos" are increasing or diminishing over time. Harold S. Kushner writes,

> I asked a friend of mine, an accomplished physicist, whether from a scientific perspective the world was becoming a more orderly place, whether randomness was increasing or decreasing with time. He replied by citing the second law of thermodynamics: every system left to itself will change in such a way as to approach equilibrium. He explained this meant that the world was changing in the direction of more randomness. Think of a group of marbles in a jar, carefully arranged by size and color. The more you shake the jar, the more that neat arrangement will give way to random distribution, until it will be only a coincidence to find one marble next to another of the same color."[7]

This, he told Rabbi Kushner, was what was happening to the world. The reply disturbed Kushner, who was told that "if it made him feel any better, Albert Einstein had the same problem. Einstein was uncomfortable with quantum physics and tried for years to disprove it, because it based itself on the hypothesis of things happening at random. Einstein preferred to believe that 'God does not play dice with the cosmos.'"[8] The conclusion this dynamic interpretation of the natural worldview seems to suggest is that God may not play dice with the cosmos, but the cosmos seems quite willing to play dice with God!

I further elaborated these worldviews, to include the monistic and the nondualistic—distinguishing between the two—and to hyphenate the theistic with the moral worldview out of deference for the widespread belief in God and God's association with morality. Now if one's imagination were allowed to play with geometrical configurations, my theodicean exploration could be represented as a chart divisible in the middle into two cones. To the more imaginative it would bring to mind a pyramid, along with its reflection, in the limpid waters of a Nile on a moonlit night. In a sense my theodicies are conical theodicies: if the central plane is constituted by the theistic-cum-moral worldview, then as one descends down the lower cone or triangle, the problem of suffering becomes less acute as we step down from the theistic-moral to the purely moral, rational, and natural planes. Hence the narrowing of the triangle. Similarly, as we move above the plane from a theistic-cum-moral worldview to a monistic and then to a nondualistic plane, the problem of suffering again diminishes in dimension, which once again explains the narrowing of the triangle, this time in the upward rather than the downward dimension. It seems that while I was physically in the hospital, my psyche maintained its equilibrium, or tried to, by functioning at the level of the natural worldview; that during my discharges and the consequent recoveries—both when inadequate and adequate—I was trying to find my philosophical feet as I stepped into the other worldviews, and that when I felt I had recovered I seemed to stand at times on the nondualistic zenith (when not in pain), and at times at the lowest point of the mirror image, the natural nadir (when in pain)!

Monistic and nondualistic worldviews

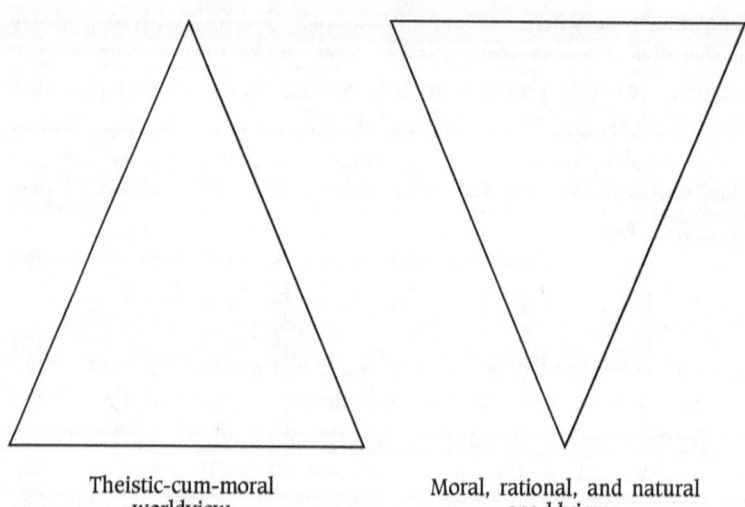

Theistic-cum-moral worldview

Moral, rational, and natural worldviews

V

We were having a rushed dinner at the Alis Plaza Hotel in Kansas City during the annual meeting of the American Academy of Religion (1991). As I finished explaining the lower part of my three-tier "theodicy" to Elaine Pagels, she said, "When our son Mark died this is how my husband made sense of it. He was a physicist and subatomic physicists deal in probabilistic theories. Our son died of a rare form of cancer which has a certain rate of incidence in a given population. Someone had to be affected and it just happened to be our son. Wouldn't the Buddhists, for instance, consider such an event as natural, as in the story of the mustard seed?"

I had to interject to make sure we both were on the same page: "The one in which the young mother, whose son has died, goes from door to door to fetch mustard seeds from a house where no one has died, because it will magically revive her son?"

"Precisely. She finds no house in which no one has died and comes to accept the death of her son as a natural fact."

I was to think about it a lot later. It seemed as if, in the course of the religious history of India during the Upanishadic age and after, the idea of karma itself had gone through three phases of the typology developed earlier in terms of three-tier theodicy comprising the lower cone: moral, rational, and natural. I could say (when my colleagues in the study of comparative religions were not listening) that perhaps the Upanishadic view of karma tended to be moral. The early Buddhist view was perhaps rational, as it accepted suffering as the result of either moral or physical causes—a determination so subtle that none other than the Buddha could be relied on to make it.[9] The Indian materialists, of course, who are the first to be discussed in the Age of Systems that follows the Buddha, adopted a natural worldview. It is not certain whether their priority in the Age of Systems is logical or chronological, but there they were, denying any transcendence of nature or immanence in nature, except for its own laws. "That is, things are what they are; and their nature, by itself, explains all the variety of the universe and the order that is noticeable in it."[10] It was one of those grand generalizations, so neat and beautiful in its sweep, that even to subject it to scrutiny seemed like betrayal. Alas—despite Keats's passionate plea—truth and beauty do not always coincide, at least not in the academia. But I digress.

VI

Elaine Pagels was writing a book about the Devil at the time. "I am adopting an attitude of agnosticism regarding his existence," she said, "in order to do the topic phenomenological justice. But we have to talk about God."

Indeed. God had to be taken into account sooner or later, and perhaps sooner rather than later. I looked at the watch to make sure we had time to talk and she would not be late for Professor Helmut Kester's lecture, which she wanted to go to. It was by someone from whom I had learned what little of New Testament exegesis a Hindu could.

"We have time," she reassured me. "God willing," I should have added, given the context. In any case I proceeded as follows: "A theistic and monistic extension of my scheme is possible, but the former complicates the issue and the latter eliminates it."

"Explain," she said gently.

"If God is factored in as a superintendent of morality, and God is good and benevolent, then the problem of suffering requires a theodicy. As has often been asked: why would a benevolent God permit suffering to exist? This is how my scheme is complicated by taking God into consideration. As you are doubtless familiar with the Christian discussions, let me give you the Hindu angle. Gandhi said that to understand why evil exists we have to be God."

"And that we can't be," Elaine Pagels said.

"But not according to Hinduism," I was compelled to add. We burst out laughing. My comment was actually unfair, because Gandhi did not subscribe to the view that we could be God, but the fact had to be taken into account that this was indeed possible according to some forms of Hinduism.[11] (Truth be told, I used to be an atheist till I embarked on the study of nondualistic Hinduism and realized that I was God!)

I did not know this at the time and only learned later that Hindu theism of the traditional Gandhian type does provide some answers. They are, however, not given by Gandhi but by Ramakrishna, the great nineteenth-century theistic mystic:

> Is evil real or unreal? What is its relation to God? Why is it not subdued by the Omnipotent? Does not its independent existence imply a dualism in the governance of the world? We have endless discussions of these questions. Sri Ramakrishna says in simple language, "Evil exists in God as poison in a serpent." What is poison to us is no poison to the serpent, but a natural secretion. The serpent does not die of its own poison. On the other hand, the secretion is a sign of its health. So evil is evil only from the point of view of man. What he regards as evil is nothing of the kind from the point of view of God. In other words, from the absolute standpoint there is no evil. But, from the relative standpoint, evil is a terrible reality and has a vital function in the spiritual economy of the world.[12]

I was prepared to go along until the last sentence, which hit me with some force, that evil has "a vital function in the spiritual economy of the world." The question that has been bothering many philosophers in the world today is that of what is called "surplus evil"—the amount of excessive evil that seems to be required to let the universe function as a system. Indeed, even the Hindu texts explain the universe emerging from Brahman as sparks fly from a fire, as hair grows on a head, conveying a sense of luxuriance and plethora rather than economy, which is conveyed by the other similes, such as that of the web spun by the spider from within itself. There could be a glut of evil in the spiritual economy of the world as well. It may be that the universe, when depicted as emerging from the impersonal Brahman, predictably contains a sense of fullness, even an overflowingness, rather than economy with no personal God in control as it were, although even here the way God answers Job is more in line with the impersonal Brahman in relation to the world. In any case: Is the spiritual economy a free economy or a planned economy? Who is to tell? It is as if the ideas of karma and *lila* do not coincide. Karma is like a planned economy, *lila* is like the free market.

Our discussion, however, had moved quickly to the monistic view, for I had added: "According to the monistic view there is really no suffering."

"How can that be?"

"According to this view reality must always be real. Our experiences in life keep changing, so they, including suffering, are not real."

"The Gnostics would agree," Elaine Pagels said; she is well known for her work on them.

"There is a less dismissive view of suffering though, one taken by a modern monistic mystic. When asked, 'Why is there suffering in the world?' he responded: 'To make you ask that question.' For such questions as: 'Who suffers? What is the ontological status of the world? What is suffering?'—such questions are extremely subversive of our normal habitual notions about ourselves and the world."

I had to use the familiar analogy of dream experience to develop the point. In a dream—let us say it is a nightmare—all that transpires comes from within us. The gorilla, the forest, and the little girl being chased by the gorilla—all have emerged out of the girl herself, who is asleep. There is the popular anecdote that the gorilla chases the little girl to the edge of a precipice in the dream. The girl stops, looks at him and asks: "What should I do now?" And he says: "I don't know, honey. It's your dream!" When the girl wakes up everything disappears—the girl alone remains.[13]

The monistic principle as such seems capable of a wider explanation. For instance, if God *alone* is what one cares for and his grace is experienced, then "When we are in grace we never mind what fruits our sins have borne. Divine forgiveness consists not in wiping out our past, but in making us indifferent to its results. We lie in the bed we made as others do; but we are wrapped in love of God that protects us."[14] Thus if *mono*theism is truly subscribed to in this sense, the problem of suffering becomes less acute. A romantic analogy might help. There is a stanza, well known to students of

Sanskrit literary criticism, that says, "Here is a person who thinks that he likes his beloved, because she does just what pleases him"; but he does not know, it adds, that "there is a higher form of love in which whatever the beloved does is, by that very fact, felt as pleasant."[15] There could similarly be two stages in one's love of God. In the first stage we love God because our prayers are answered. But in the second stage, whatever happens to us, good or bad, is equally welcome from the mere fact that it flows from God. The fact that it is God-given overwhelms the distinction of our preferences, for we prefer God, above them, as their source over them.

The same holds true when karma is accepted as the one principle that accounts for all our empirical experiences, good or bad:

> It is therefore in vain that he rejoices or is aggrieved of a happy or an unhappy event, because the decrees of Destiny are inevitable even for demons and gods. Man can never escape pleasure or pain, because his body, which is a product of his good or bad actions, is by nature transient. After pleasure pain, after pain pleasure: creatures cannot escape these two, as they cannot [escape] the succession of day and night. They are intimately associated as water and mud. It is, therefore, that Sages knowing that all is but illusion, remain steadfast and neither are aggrieved nor joyous for events unhappy and happy.[16]

Talking of karma, that reminds me—

VII

"What about karma?" Elaine Pagels had then asked. Indeed, how could it have been kept at bay for so long? Familiarity had bred contempt rather than attempt.

I tried to explain the concept to her. However, the harder I tried, the more pedantic I began to sound. Even to myself. So I stopped midstream and said, "May I tell you a story?" "Please do," she said.

"I love stories." I thereupon narrated to her the following story:

Whom Should I Mourn?

Whenever he went off to battle, a certain army officer kept his money—2,000 rupees—in trust with a Rawalpindi merchant who was under contract to supply rations to the troops. One day during the Kabul uprising, the officer was killed under bizarre circumstances: he was unable to stop the mare he was riding from heading directly into the enemy lines. No matter how hard he reined in the usually trustworthy animal, she would not alter her deadly course, and a hail of fire killed both horse and rider.

The government sent the officer's belongings to his relatives, who knew nothing about the sum of money he had left with the merchant. The merchant, for his part, mentioned the money to no one, and kept it as if it were his own.

Twenty years later he was living in Saharanpur, running a small shop. One night, as he was entertaining some old friends, his guests heard sobs and piteous cries coming from the next room. The merchant explained that this was his daughter-in-law, mourning her husband who had died only a few days before. The guests offered their condolences, but expressed surprise that the merchant was entertaining them when he, too, should be mourning his son's death. In reply, the merchant told them the following story:

"Twenty years ago, after my return from Rawalpindi, I married, and my wife gave birth to a son. When he had grown up, we arranged a marriage for him, but immediately after the wedding he became gravely ill, and nothing we did would cure him. Finally, I brought in a Muslim clergyman to try to heal him. The clergyman recited some words and I immediately gave him two and one-half rupees, which was all I had in my pocket at that moment. I then asked my son how he felt. He said that he was about to die and explained:

" 'Twenty years ago,' he told me, 'I left 2,000 rupees in your safekeeping just before I was killed in the Kabul uprising. You kept the money, and so I was reborn as your son to recover it. The two and one-half rupees you had in your pocket were all that was left of that money, and when you passed them on to the priest in payment for the services he had rendered to me, our account was squared.

" 'The mare that rode so willfully directly into enemy lines was reborn as my wife, and because of the way in which she made me die, she will have to grieve at my passing. That will square my account with her.' "

"So," the merchant said, "the officer is dead and the mare is crying. For whom should I mourn, the mare or the officer? Therefore, gentlemen, be good enough to enjoy your meal."[17]

She listened to the story intently as we enjoyed our meal and then said: "So what happens to us is the result of our own doing."

"That's the bottom line," I said.

"I would rather feel guilty than helpless," she said simply.[18]

This was an uncanny comment. Are all the various theodicies designed to do just this—make us feel guilty rather than helpless? The much-ridiculed guilt-trip of Christianity seemed to emerge in a new light. Or is it that all theodicies are designed paradoxically either to make us guilt-ridden *or* free us of guilt? That is, it is the liminal zone between them that emotionally devastates and spiritually castrates. "It is the will of God" puts it squarely in God's court, and karma in ours: the tension of the game lasts while the ball has *not* landed on either side of the court. However, even if karma enlarges the scope of our understanding of the universe, does it exhaust it?

VIII

What if we are starting with the wrong assumption? What if there is an a priori teleological bias in our thinking, this need to find meaning when there might be none?

"You know. Even my three-year-old child says, 'but this is not fair,'" I remembered Elaine Pagels telling me on the phone. I had called her to extend an invitation on behalf of our faculty a few years ago, and what I thought would be a three-minute conversation turned into a thirty-minute conversation. Snippets of that conversation began to surface as Elaine Pagels spoke again in the restaurant, now buzzing with activity but where we were having this conversation nonetheless, transcending the triviality of our daily existence.

"We may be starting at the wrong end," she said, "when we assume that there was first a paradise and then a fall. I think the Buddhists have the right starting point—life is suffering and happiness is remission."

"And indeed, why should life be fair?" I asked. "That could also be a misleading assumption. As Ann Landers says, 'Whatever it is that hits the fan, it is not distributed evenly.'"

We were really in an iconoclastic mood. It is a good thing we did not break any china. We had just thrown the teleological assumption of philosophy and the paradisiacal assumption of Christian cosmology overboard. Next to go was the didactic assumption of theodicy that suffering is the schoolmaster of spirituality. This was another false starting point.

"I am none the wiser for breaking my leg, except in crossing roads more carefully. Even there I am not so sure. The other day . . ."

"My husband died in a mountaineering accident, just when we were recovering from our son's death and had adopted a daughter . . ."

"What a creative response . . ." I said, almost involuntarily.

"My friend also thinks so. You know her, I think."

"Indeed I do." Indeed I did. Once, years ago, when the American Academy of Religion met at Dallas there was a freak snowstorm. All the attendees who had not yet departed were shepherded into the part of the hotel that was still functioning. That is when, through the congeniality that results from proximity, my professional acquaintance with the person she had in mind was transformed into personal friendship.

"We got this rare chance to adopt. We went down to see the child, a small girl, premature. I didn't like her then. On the one hand I wanted to adopt a child so badly; on the other I didn't like the child who had come up for adoption! I called our mutual friend and told her, 'My heart was breaking to pieces; what should I do?' She said: 'The Indians have a word for it: it translates as compassion.' You know that is the name she gave to her daughter."

I listened, enthralled, to this human drama.

" 'Have compassion,' she said. We adopted her and of course she's such a lovely child. So is David, the son we adopted. But did one have to suffer to do all that?"

Elaine Pagels was preaching to the converted. I think suffering rarely provides insight, more often it blurs the vision. Tears may cleanse the eye but they fog the spectacles, and most of us have them, symbolically if not literally. Natural 20/20 vision is rare.

Biblical wisdom seems to be divided on the virtuous effects of suffering. On the one hand it says, "Sorrow is better than laughter: for by the sadness of the countenance the heart is made better" (Ecclesiastes 7:3). But it also says, "By sorrow of heart the spirit is broken" (Proverbs 15:13). This, however, does a Shakespeare on the Bible, in the sense that one can be both for and against a position: what counts is the style, not the substance, unless one wishes to argue that the style is the substance. Shakespeare can, with equal eloquence, hold human beings themselves or fate responsible for their condition. However, in its overall context, although the Bible may speak with different voices, it does not speak with a forked tongue. It attaches a redemptive value to suffering as much as a punitive one, and it does attach value to suffering, though it may not make the point with the elegance of Pearl S. Buck: "There is alchemy in sorrow. It can be transmuted into wisdom."[19] However, will this hold if the affliction is so terrible as to paralyze reflection? Is not making a virtue of suffering to be distinguished from making suffering itself a virtue? Even when Hindu thought tackles the far lighter theme of performing duty for its own sake, even deontologically, it wishes to distinguish such duty from drudgery: "Disinterested activity, in the literal sense of the expression, is a psychological impossibility; and to insist on it in the name of morality is . . . to reduce it to a form of meaningless drudgery."[20] Abraham Joshua Heschel observes, "It is usually in the wake of frustration, in moments of crisis and self-disillusionment, and rarely out of astonishment at man's glorious achievement, that radical reflection comes to pass."[21] I offer then the radical reflection here: why have things to come to such a pass? Many people, it is true, are religious only in moments of crisis. There is, of course, an existential element in this, but a sociological element can be discerned as well: have we been socialized into believing that agony is a more effective schoolmaster than ecstasy? Perhaps this view of suffering arises from the notion, as Gordon W. Allport says, that "religion itself is ultimately a loving hope; a hope that . . . there is a God, that there is meaning in human suffering and in the disappointment of our individual, self-centered hopes."[22]

Hope. Wouldn't reasonable expectation be better? Is suffering the surgeon's lancet or the butcher's blade? At least at the time of that conversation, both Professor Pagels and I were more disposed to the latter view of it.

I must now recall further the earlier discussion we had on the phone, although it plays one extreme end of the spectrum against the other. I had told her of the precognitive dream of Stephanie. "What if everything is predetermined?" I had said.

"By whom?"

"At this stage that does not matter. By God, karma, fate, whatever. If everything is predetermined then the problem reduces itself from that of the *existence* of suffering to that of the *acceptance* of suffering. Once, of course, we raise the question of how, why, or by what it is predetermined, the old questions arise again. But what I found interesting was that once I entertained the idea of predetermination per se, I immediately became less anxious in my existential situation. So it is a useful anxiolytic strategy."

"But is it true?"

"We don't know. But if in a given situation we cannot determine the *truth* of an answer, then should we not be guided by its value?"

"What do you mean?"

"Let us take the question of free will. If we cannot definitely determine whether free will exists or not, does it not make sense to ask: what results follow if we *assume* it does and then *assume* it does not, and depending on which assumption is conducive to more wholesome results, act *as if* free will existed or did not, depending on which of the assumptions was more conducive to well-being."

"I find the idea of acting *as if* totally bankrupt and hollow," she said.

Elaine Pagels had said this with such force that I dared not narrate my experience of acting for two weeks *as if* everything were predetermined and the three striking results it produced: (1) I was cheerful all the time, (2) I could not harbor any ill will toward anybody, but (3) my productivity dropped—a development that friends of mine who complain that I publish too much (compared to whom?) would have welcomed. I didn't continue with the experiment. But I recall, and can still recall, the awe I felt when compelled to entertain the possibility, as a result of my own personal experiences, that not just the thoughts we think but the emotions we *feel* may be predetermined. And what difference, one may well ask, could such a realization make to those feelings? One can only say this: that one did not get excited about getting excited and feel depressed about feeling depressed.

The explanation from destiny must appear so antiquated to the modern mind at first sight that its prevalence must initially be documented, whether one's undoing is one's own doing or that of some other power. Marcus Aurelius's statement is the most sweeping in this respect: "Whatever befalls thee was preordained to thee from eternity."[23] It is also the most economical: what happens to us within time is explained to us in terms of Time itself. For Mencius, Heaven ordained it and "Everything is destiny."[24] In Judaism, too, things are ordained from on high, but by one on high: "A man does not hurt his finger unless it is decreed from above" (Talmud, Hullin 7).[25] Christianity and Islam are as explicit in calling it God.

As the sparrow falls on the earth it follows a divinely known and perhaps also divinely determined trajectory, the Gospels assure us: "There will nothing befall us but that God hath written down for us" (Qur'n 9:51).[26]

Western theology and philosophy take the cue. John Calvin declares, "There is no such thing as fortune or chance. . . . God's children . . . are governed by God's secret plan in such a way that nothing happens except what is knowingly and willingly decreed by Him."[27] Spinoza strikes a predictably more philosophical note: "All things have been predestined by God, not indeed . . . from an absolutely arbitrary decree, but from the absolute nature or infinite power of God."[28]

Sidney Greenberg (*Say Yes to Life*), however, offers the most powerful existential argument in favor of free will as follows: "The most compelling reason no one can predict the future is that the future does not exist. You and I are not robots. We have freedom of will to determine the shape of tomorrow by what we do today."[29] It is a pity that the argument, as such, can only hold for a linear view of time. Nevertheless the discussion of destiny is not without its element of free choice: "God asks no man whether he will accept life. That is not the choice. You must take it. The only choice is *how*."[30]

However, the tension persists. On the one hand Schopenhauer can ask, "A man can do what he wills but can he will what he wills?" On the other, Anselm can remark, "God hath promised pardon to him that repenteth, but he has not promised repentance to him that sinneth." And I myself was destined to experience this tension repeatedly and must wonder both whether I had transcended it and whether it can be transcended.

IX

It is the Hindu philosophy of nondualism that seems to do away with all the three horns of the trilemma: with God, with God's activity in the universe, and with the individual and his or her suffering. For according to this system, in the final analysis neither God nor the universe nor you nor I exist—to say nothing of suffering!

This standpoint is unique and difficult to explain. A modern exponent of this school, Ramana Maharshi (d. 1950), for instance, declares that on the path to the knowledge of ultimate reality, "Isvara, God, the creator, the personal God is the last of unreal forms to go."[31] He also comments, "What is the meaning of this talk of truth and falsehood in the world which is itself false?"[32] and makes short shrift of suffering by stating that "like the unreal blueness of the sky, misery does not exist in reality but only in mere imagination"[33]—it is unreal.

When explained in so succinct a manner, this perspective on suffering, although it might pique our curiosity, is merely tantalizing, if one does not discard it as bizarre. Psychologists might even say that such people are in denial in a big way. One must therefore present its unusual perspective more comprehensively. We begin by recognizing that "the paradoxes inherent in theistic theories have engaged the minds of western theologians for centuries. For example, if God is perfect, why is there evil in the world? Why does an omnipotent God allow suffering when he has the power to abolish it at a stroke?"[34] One way to solve the problem at one stroke is to attribute all suffering to a factor other than God—namely the Devil—and to resolve the issue through a frank dualism.

The other approach, adopted here, is to solve it by resorting to a frank monism (or more accurately, nondualism) that eliminates not suffering but its *reality*. "All the present troubles are due to thoughts and are themselves thoughts."[35] According to this view, God, the universe, and the individual are all unreal, and so is suffering: "The world, the individual soul and God are appearances" in the ultimate reality, "like silver in mother-of-pearl; these appear at the same time and disappear at the same time."[36]

In Ramana's thought, the words "mind" and "ego" play a key role: "The ego and the mind are the same,"[37] and "thoughts alone constitute the mind."[38] Now: "All religions first postulate three principles, the world, the soul and God. To say that one principle alone appears as the three principles or that the three principles are always three principles is possible only so long as the ego exists."[39]

The problems, paradoxes, or conundrums associated with theodicies involve these three elements, but Ramana Maharshi "sidesteps such conundrums by stating that the world, God and the individual who suffers are all inventions of the mind."[40]

For suffering to exist there must be some*one* who suffers. Ramana maintains that such individuality is illusory. David Godman offers the following useful summary of his position on suffering:

> Instead of attributing suffering to the consequence of wrong actions or to the will of God, Sri Ramana taught that it only arises because we imagine that we are separate individuals interacting with each other and with the world. He said that *wrong actions compound the suffering, and are therefore to be avoided, but they are not its original cause*. It is the mind that creates the illusion of separateness and it is the mind that suffers the consequences of its illusory inventions. Suffering is thus a product and consequence of the discriminative mind; when the mind is eliminated, suffering is found to be non-existent.[41]

He goes on to add,

> Many questioners could relate to this idea on an individual level but they found it hard to accept that all the suffering in the world existed only in the mind of the person who perceived it. Sri Ramana was quite adamant about this and he repeatedly said that if one realises the Self, one will know that all suffering, not just one's own, is non-existent. Taking this idea to its logical conclusion, Sri Ramana often said the most effective way of eliminating other people's suffering was to realise the Self.[42]

The point that must be firmly borne in mind in this discussion is that for this school of thought, all suffering is only contextual rather than real, just as pain is real in a nightmare but unreal outside of that context. This school thus offers a radical ontological theodicy: without denying the *existence* of suffering, it denies its *reality*.⁴³ The most conclusive evidence comes from the life of Ramana himself. He had a follower named Echammal, who "Before she was twenty-five . . . lost her husband, her only son, and finally her only daughter, in quick succession."⁴⁴ She started serving him after leaving her home and with his "concurrence . . . adopted a girl . . . as her foster daughter," "got her married," and had a grandson.⁴⁵ Then the adopted daughter suddenly died. "So she ran up to the Maharshi and handed him the telegram. *As he read it he wept.*"⁴⁶ When the baby of the departed daughter arrived she "placed him in the arms of the Maharshi. *Again he burst into tears . . .*"⁴⁷

This is truly an extraordinary theodicy perhaps meant for extraordinary people; I'm not one of them. For an ordinary person like me it is too subversive of ordinary modes of existence—it offered a challenge when I was perhaps looking for comfort. This combination of the very real existential sympathy felt by Ramana Maharshi for the suffering of others, with his metaphysical certainty of its nonreality, represents an astonishing blend of compassion and wisdom. It has been made famous by Buddhism and is not without a certain appeal for a certain type of person, or for any type of person in a certain frame of mind, but I could not frame my worldview in it, though I was bewitched for a while by the picture it presented. What if our experiences are really on par with dreams? What if the world *is* but a dream, which seems to be the moral of the following parable?

> A son was born to a king. He was the only child and was therefore "the apple of the eye" of both the king and the queen. The prince became a favourite with all and as he grew older he was taught all the arts and the sciences. One day, all of a sudden, the prince fell ill. The malady went on getting worse and even the best physician of the kingdom found that all treatments were of no avail. Both the king and the queen never left his side day and night and the most competent physician and nurses continuously attended on him. The king was exhausted by his constant vigil and one night he could not resist falling asleep. He was awakened by the sound of crying

and weeping and learnt that the prince had passed away while he was he was asleep. The king sat as if he was stupefied, without speaking a single word. The queen asked him how it was that on the passing away of the only child whom he loved so much there was not a single drop of tear in his eyes. The king said, "Oh queen, when I fell asleep I dreamt that I had become the monarch of a large kingdom, much larger than mine, and the father of seven worthy and ideal princes, each of whom was well trained in the art of administration. I handed over the charge of my kingdom to them and thereafter I was spending my days in peace and happiness with you. And now this tragedy has taken place and I am unable to make up my mind whether I should lament for the child that has left us today or whether I should mourn the loss of the seven sons and a vast kingdom. I see no difference in the two bereavements and to me the world has become nothing but a dream."[48]

Once Ramana was asked whether one in his state felt "any physical pain, say, of a sting or a cut?" He replied: "All pains, even physical, are in the mind. Everybody feels the pain of a cut or a sting, but the *Jnani*, whose mind is sunk in bliss, feels it *as in a dream*. His resembles the case of the two lovers in the story who were tortured together but did not feel pain because their minds were in ecstasy, gazing at each other's face."[49]

But life was not a dream for me. A part of it was spent in dreaming but it was not a dream.

X

If the wisdom of India had, at least so far, failed to provide a satisfactory answer, what about China, a civilization as old and great as that of India? It is perhaps only the vestige of my past nationalism that now prevents me from describing it as a civilization "older" and "greater" than that of India. Had not the Prophet exhorted one to seek knowledge, which we might deliberately overinterpret as wisdom in the present context—even from China? At first I hesitated. Is not China's greatest cultural failure ideological, just as India's is linguistic? It is not that India does not have its own language (Sanskrit) or languages (too many to enumerate), but its linguistic landscape from the twelfth century onward has been dominated by languages of foreign origin—the remotest and most recent being English. Similarly, it is not that China has not had its own systems of thought, such as Confucianism and Taoism, but that it is more prone to ideological penetration by foreign systems such as Buddhism and now Marxism. Just as, despite the vicissitudes of history, India has somehow managed to cling to its religion, Hinduism, China has succeeded in doing the same with regard to its language, Chinese.

Such intellectual scruples, however, which now even appear petty, were swept away by the rising tide of a search for meaning. Taoism came to mind first and it came to mind immediately, for it provided two anecdotes that involved a broken leg and a departed spouse, the incidents that had brought me and Elaine Pagels together in our quest for meaning. The incident of the broken leg appears midstream in the following account in the *Hua Nan Tzu*, a Chinese classic, which I am told has yet to be translated into English in its entirety.

> A poor farmer's horse ran off into the country of the barbarians. All his neighbors offered their condolences, but his father said, "How do you know that this isn't good fortune?" After a few months the horse returned with a barbarian horse of excellent stock. All his neighbors offered their congratulations, but his father said, "How do you know that this isn't a disaster?" The two horses bred, and the family became rich in fine horses. *The farmer's son spent much of his time riding them; one day he fell off and broke his hipbone.* All his neighbors offered the farmer their condolences but his father said, "How do you know that this isn't good fortune?" Another

year passed, and the barbarians invaded the frontier. All the able-bodied young men were conscripted, and nine-tenths of them died in the war. Thus good fortune can be disaster and vice versa. Who can tell how events will be transformed?[50]

The farmer's son was saved from conscription by his broken leg.[51] What was I saved from? This is the great mystery! One would never know. It is like the perfect genocide in which *every* member of the genus is killed. No one lives to tell the tale. It is as if it never occurred. How does one know the being of nonbeing, the happening of nonhappening when it does not happen? Is cosmic confidence in the rightness of things somehow the only cure for doubt? A modern Hindu woman saint of the twentieth century, Anandamayi Ma, once said, "Many have been saved from calamity by adversity." But how do we know? And as this Sufi story informs us, the penalty of asking more questions may come in the form of a deeper silence from across the table. The story is about Khadir or Khizr,

> a mysterious sage endowed with immortality, who is said to enter into conversation with wandering Sufis and impart to them his God-given knowledge. Moses desired to accompany him on a journey that he might profit by his teaching, and Khadir consented, only stipulating that Moses should ask no questions of him.
> So they both went on, till they embarked in a boat and he (Khadir) staved it in. "What!" cried Moses, "hast thou staved it in that thou mayst drown its crew? Verily, a strange thing hast thou done."
> He said, "Did not I tell thee that thou couldst no way have patience with me?"
> Then they went on until they met a youth, and he slew him. Said Moses, "Hast thou slain him who is free from guilt of blood? Surely now thou hast wrought an unheard-of thing!"After Moses had broken his promise of silence for the third time, Khadir resolved to leave him.

"But first," he said, "I will tell thee the meaning of that with which thou couldst not have patience. As to the boat, it belonged to poor men, toilers on the sea, and I was minded to damage it, for in their rear was a king who seized on every boat by force. And as to the youth, his parents were believers, and I feared lest he should trouble them by error and unbelief."[52]

Who knows. Maybe Khadir is a Taoist immortal.

Chuang Tzu's wife died. When Hui Tzu went to convey his condolences, he found Chuang Tzu sitting with his legs sprawled out, pounding on a tub and singing. "You lived with her, she brought up your children and grew old." said Hui Tzu. "It should be enough simply not to weep at her death. But pounding on a tub and singing—this is going too far, isn't it?"

Chuang Tzu said, "You're wrong. When she first died, do you think I didn't grieve like anyone else? But I looked back to her beginning and the time before she was born. Not only the time before she was born, but the time before she had a body. Not only the time before she had a body, but the time before she had a spirit. In the midst of the jumble of wonder and mystery a change took place and she had a spirit. Another change and she had a body. Another change and she was born. Now there's been another change and she's dead. It's just like the progression of the four seasons, spring, summer, fall, winter."

"Now she's going to lie down peacefully in a vast room. If I were to follow after her bawling and sobbing, it would show that I don't understand anything about fate. So I stopped."[53]

Perhaps the philosophy underlying Chuang Tzu's attitude toward the death of his wife is more fully articulated in another part of the work that bears his name, in which a disciple discusses his attitude toward the passing away of Lao Tan, another name for Lao Tzu:

> When Lao Tan died, Ch'in Shih went to mourn for him; but after giving three cries, he left the room.
> "Weren't you a friend of the Master?" asked Lao Tzu's disciples.
> "Yes."
> "And you think it's all right to mourn him this way?"
> "Yes," said Ch'in Shih. "At first I took him for a real man, but now I know he wasn't. A little while ago, when I went in to mourn, I found old men weeping for him as though they were weeping for a son, and young men weeping for him as though they were weeping for a mother. To have gathered a group like *that*, he must have done something to make them talk about him, though he didn't ask them to talk, or make them weep for him, though he didn't ask them to weep. This is to hide from Heaven, turn your back on the true state of affairs, and forget what you were born with. In the old days, this was called the crime of hiding from Heaven. Your master happened to come because it was his time, and he happened to leave because things follow along. If you are content with the time and willing to follow along, then grief and joy have no way to enter in. In the old days, this was called being freed from the bonds of God."[54]

One could certainly accept death as the counterpart of life, if it did one the courtesy of coming about naturally and not by accident. It is not just death but accidental death that provokes the sharp quest for meaning; it is not a natural illness but an accidental injury that raises the question: why? My knee did not buckle under the weight of years; it collapsed as a result of a collision. And how is that to be explained naturally, except perhaps probabilistically?

The answers that arose from Taoism in response to the question were fascinating rather than satisfying, and not altogether unfamiliar once divested of their Chinese guise. Could it be that Confucianism held more promise? I knew it had been said of Confucius, "Oh, is he the one who knows that it cannot be done and still does it?"[55] What I did not know, until my friend Liu Xiaogan from Beijing told me, was that this spirit was reflected, for example, in Tso Ch'iu-ming's firm resolution to compile the first Chinese Chronicle (*Tso Chuan*) *after* he became blind, and Ssu-ma Ch'ien's completion of his first biographical history (*Shih-Chi*) *after* he was castrated by the imperial court as a punishment. He also cited the example of Ch'u Yuan, a poet who threw himself into a river because he had failed to gain the king's ear to protest an impenetrable bureaucracy and ended his life in this somewhat Kafkaesque (rather than Quixotic) manner.

The point then seemed to be not that I had broken my leg, but what had I gone on to accomplish given the fact that I had broken my leg, or *despite* it. This is a laudable, an admirable response, with a philosophy to go with it;[56] however, it is a response, it is not an answer. It tells us how to give meaning *to* life; does it tell us the meaning of life, or death?

XI

We have talked of God, but what about Satan? Swami Vivekananda was destined to proudly proclaim to the world in his later years that "there is no Satan in Hinduism."[57] However, when in the throes of a personal crisis brought on by the sudden death of his father through cardiac arrest, he had begun to wonder whether the world had not "been created by a demon."[58] An account of the suffering that led him to such a conclusion must be included at this point in some detail, not only for completeness of description but to permit full comprehension of the issues involved.

> I went about hither and thither in search of a job even before the period of mourning [due to the passing away of his father] was over. Suffering from lack of food, I was going barefooted from office to office with an

application for a job in my hand in the blazing midday sun. Sympathising with me in my sorrow, some of my very intimate friends would be with me some days, but on other days they could not be. But I had to be disappointed everywhere. From that very first worldly experience of mine I felt keenly that selfless sympathy was very rare in this world—there was no place here for the weak and the poor. Those who deemed it, only a day or two previously, a piece of good fortune to be able to help me now found an opportunity to do the contrary and made a wry face at me, and although able, were reluctant to help me. When I had such experiences, the world seemed to me, very often, to have been created by a demon. One day, at that time, when I was going from place to place in the sun, my sole, I remember, was blistered. Extremely fatigued, I had to sit down in the shade of the Ochterloney monument in the Maidan. A friend or two were with me that day or met me there by chance. One of them, I remember distinctly, sang by way of consoling me—

"Here blows the wind, the breath of Brahman,
His grace palpable. . . ."

When I heard the song I felt as if he was inflicting severe blows on my head. Remembering the sheer helpless condition of my mother and brothers, I blurted out in resentment, despair and disappointment, "Shut up. Those who are in the lap of luxury or do not know what the pinch of hunger means, and whose nearest and dearest ones are not starving and going naked—to such people, in the midst of the fullest enjoyment of life, such flights of imagination appear sweet and pleasing. I also had such days and felt similarly, but now, confronted with stern reality, all these sentiments seem to be a terrible mockery."

In spite of all my trials, my faith in the existence of God did not vanish so long, for all that pain and misery, nor did I doubt that "God is good." I used to wake up from sleep in the morning, remembered the Lord and left my bed taking His name. Then with firm determination and hope I went from place to place in search of some means of earning money. I was leaving my bed as usual, calling on the Lord, when one day, my mother heard my words from the adjacent room and suddenly said, "Stop, lad; you have been constantly repeating the name of the divine Lord ever since your childhood—and your divine Lord has left nothing undone!" The words hurt me terribly. Cut to the quick, I pondered, "Does God actually exist? If so, does He hear the plaintive prayer of man? Why is there then no response to so much of prayer which I proffer to Him? Whence is so much of evil in the creation of a benign Creator? Why is there so much of calamity in the kingdom of one who is all Bliss?" . . . My heart was pierced through by a feeling of wounded love; and doubt in the existence of God assailed me.

It was against my nature to do anything and conceal it from others. Never from my childhood could I conceal, out of fear or from any other motive, even the least shade of thought, let alone my actions. Was it, therefore, surprising that I should now go aggressively forward to prove to the people that God did not exist and, even if he did, there was no need to call on Him, for it produced no result to do so? Consequently, a rumour soon spread that I had become an atheist and was mixing with people of bad character, did not shrink from drinking and even from frequenting the houses of ill-fame.[59]

The case of Vivekananda parallels the account of the sufferings of Job and even the answer Job got from God. Ronald M. Green places the Book of Job in its historical context and notes that the "simple equation between suffering and punishment" as articulated in Isaiah 3:10–11 did not go unchallenged in biblical thinking, and the disasters of the period from the Babylonian exile onward, when the Israelites were often most intensely loyal to the covenant, forced an explanation of seemingly innocent suffering. In wisdom literature, especially the Book of Job, the older theodicy is rejected. Job is an innocent man, blameless and righteous in every way; yet he suffers (Job 1–2). The prose epilogue, apparently appended at a later date, seeks to maintain the retributive schema by suggesting that Job is eventually more than compensated for his trials (42:10–17), but the book's most decisive response to suffering borders on a radical dissolution of the theodicy problem. Answering Job out of a whirlwind, God asks, "Where were you when I laid the foundations of the earth?" (38:4). A litany of God's mighty deeds in nature and history follows, with the suggestion that man is too puny a creature to question his maker's justice. Job repents his presumption: "I have uttered what I did not understand, things too wonderful for me, which I did not know" (42:3).[60]

The case of Vivekananda represents a slight variation of this theme. It is not the puniness of a human being in the face of God but the realization of the puniness of self-serving prayers of a human being when face to face with God that drives home the lesson difficult even to comprehend, much less to learn. We resume the narrative of Vivekananda's suffering at the appropriate point to bring it to its conclusion:

> . . . a hundred thoughts about the family occupied my mind. I began going from place to place now as before and made various kinds of efforts. I worked in the office of the attorney and translated a few books, as a result of which I earned a little money and the household was being managed somehow. But these were all temporary jobs; and in the absence of any permanent work no smooth arrangement for the maintenance of mother and brothers could be made. I remembered a little later: "God grants the Master's prayers. I shall make him pray for me so that the suffering of my mother and brothers for want of food and clothing might be removed; he will never refuse to do so for my sake." I hurried to Dakshineswar and

THE AFTERMATH: THE SEARCH FOR MEANING / 71

asked persistently that he must pray to the Mother that the pecuniary difficulty of my mother and brothers might be removed. The Master said to me affectionately, "My child, I cannot say such words, you know. Why don't you yourself pray? You don't accept the Mother; that is why you suffer so much." I replied, "I have no knowledge of the Mother; please pray to Mother yourself for my sake. Pray you must; I will not leave you unless you do so." The Master said with affection, "I prayed to Mother many times indeed to remove your sufferings. But as you do not accept Mother, She does not grant the prayer. Well today is Tuesday, a day especially sacred to Mother. Mother will, I say, grant you whatever you would ask for. Go to the temple tonight and, bowing down to Her, pray for a boon. My affectionate Mother is the Power of Brahman; She is pure Consciousness embodied. She has given birth to the universe according to Her will; what can She not do, if she wills?"

    A firm faith arose in my mind that all the sufferings would certainly come to an end as soon as I prayed to the Mother, inasmuch as the Master had said so. I waited for the night in great expectancy. The night arrived at last. Three hours of the night had elapsed when the Master asked me to go to the holy temple. As I was going, a sort of profound inebriation possessed me; I was reeling. A firm conviction gripped me that I should actually see Mother and hear Her words. I forgot all other things, and became completely merged in that thought alone. Coming in the temple, I saw that Mother was actually pure Consciousness, was actually living and was really the fountain-head of infinite love and beauty. My heart swelled with loving devotion; and, beside myself with bliss, I made repeated salutations to Her, praying, "Mother, grant me discrimination, grant me detachment, grant me divine knowledge and devotion; ordain that I may always have unobstructed vision of you." My heart was flooded with peace. The whole universe completely disappeared and Mother alone remained filling my heart.

No sooner had I returned to the Master than he asked, "Did you pray to Mother for the removal of your worldly wants?" Startled at his question, I said, "No sir; I forgot to do so. So, what should I do now?" He said, "Go quickly again and pray to Her." I started for the temple once more, and, coming to Mother's presence, became inebriated again. I forgot everything, bowed down to Her repeatedly and prayed for the realization of divine knowledge and devotion, before I came back. The Master smiled and said, "Well, did you tell Her this time?" I was startled again and said, "No, sir; hardly had I seen Mother when I forgot everything on account of the influence of an indescribably divine Power and prayed for knowledge and devotion only. What's to be done now?" The Master said, "Silly boy, could you not control yourself a little and make that prayer? Go once more, if you can and tell Her those words. Quick!" I started a third time; but as soon as I entered the temple a formidable sense of shame occupied my heart. I thought what a trifling thing have I come to ask of Mother? It is, as the Master says, just the folly of asking a king, having received his grace, for gourds and pumpkins. Ah! how low is my intellect! Overpowered with shame and aversion I bowed down to Her over and over again saying, "I don't want anything else, Mother; do grant me divine knowledge and devotion only." When I came out from the temple, it occurred to me that it was certainly the play of the Master, otherwise how was it that I could not speak the words though I came to pray to Her as many as three times? Afterwards I insisted that he must ensure my mother's and brothers' freedom from lack of food and clothing, saying, "It is certainly you who made me intoxicated that way." He said affectionately to me, "My child, I can never offer such a prayer for anyone; it does not indeed come out of my mouth. You would, I told you, get from Mother whatever you wanted. But you could not ask Her for it; you are not meant for worldly happiness. What am I to do?" I said, "That won't do, sir. You must utter the prayer for my sake; it is my firm conviction that they will be free from all sufferings if you only say so." As I kept on persisting, he said, "Well, they will never be in want of plain food and clothing."[61]

Some differences from Job's experiences are apparent. In this case the Goddess rather than God is addressed; Vivekananda is not "more than compensated" for his trials, though the family is perhaps taken care of—a minimalist response rather than a maximalist one, as in the case of Job. The Goddess does not lecture Vivekananda the way God lectured Job, and though Job has friends, like Vivekananda, unlike Vivekananda he does not have a Master (who continued to influence Vivekananda's life posthumously by his presence).[62] There is, however, a fundamental similarity in the human inability to comprehend divine majesty and perhaps even divine justice: "The *Book of Job* may be read as an abandonment of the very effort to comprehend God's justice, as an assertion that a creature cannot ask its maker to render account. Or, less radically, it may be read as a deferred theodicy—not the claim that God is unjust or beyond justice but that we are unprepared here and now to fathom God's righteous ways. The repeated assertions of God's control of the wicked support this interpretation."[63] Vivekananda's experience can be read in similar ways. To seek financial gain from God or the Goddess even in an impecunious state in His or Her presence was "just like the folly of asking a king, having received his grace, for gourds and pumpkins."[64] There is however a curious inversion here compared with Job: Vivekananda cannot render his account to God, whereas Job cannot ask God to render his account. In both cases, however, the difficulty arises on account of the disparity of the relative status of God and his creature, a disparity so great as to possess a dimension of mystery.

Nor is the sense of mystery diminished by these encounters. In the case of the Bible, Ronald Green goes on to observe, "In any case, the more radical stance, amounting to a dissolution of the theodicy problem, finds expression elsewhere in the wisdom literature. Ecclesiastes, for example, repeatedly emphasizes the obscurity of God's ways in dealing with man. Occasionally the text despairs of there being any justice in the world: 'one fate comes to all, to the righteous and the wicked, to the good and the evil'" (Ecclesiastes 9:2).[65] And Swami Vivekananda was destined to state in one of his conversations later in life, which occurred on May 1, 1897:

> **Swamiji:** . . . Unless He makes us understand, nothing can be stated or understood. Somebody comes to the fullest faith even without seeing or hearing, while somebody else remains plunged in doubt even after witnessing with his own eyes various extraordinary powers for twelve years! The secret of it all is His grace! But then one must persevere, so that the grace may be received.
>
> **Disciple:** Is there, sir, any law of grace?
>
> **Swamiji:** Yes and no.
>
> **Disciple:** How is that?
>
> **Swamiji:** Those who are pure always in body, mind, and speech, who have strong devotion, who discriminate between the real and the unreal, who persevere in meditation and contemplation—upon them alone the grace of the Lord descends. The Lord, however, is beyond all natural laws—is not under any rules and regulations, or just as Shri Ramakrishna used to say, He has the child's nature—and that's why we find some failing to get any response even after calling on Him for millions of births, while some one else whom we regard as a sinful or penitent man or a disbeliever, would have Illumination in a flash!—On the latter the Lord perhaps lavishes His grace

quite unsolicited! You may argue that this man had good merits stored up from previous life, but the mystery is really difficult to understand. Shri Ramakrishna used to say sometimes, "Do rely on Him; be like the dry leaf at the mercy of the wind"; and again he would say, "The wind of His grace is always blowing, what you need to do is to unfurl your sail."

Disciple: But, sir, this is a most tremendous statement. No reasoning, I see, can stand here.

Swamiji: Ah, all reasoning and arguing is within the limit of the realm of Maya; it lies within the categories of space, time, and causation. But He is beyond these categories. We speak of His law, still He is beyond all law. He creates, or becomes, all that we speak of as laws of nature, and yet He is outside of them all. He on whom His grace descends, in a moment goes beyond all law. For this reason there is no condition in grace. It is as His play or sport. And this creation of the universe is like His play—"It is the pure delight of sport, as in the case of men" (*Vedanta-Sutra* II. i. 33). It is not possible for Him who creates and destroys the universe as if in play to grant salvation by grace to the greatest sinner? But then it is just His pleasure, His play, to get somebody through the practice of spiritual discipline and somebody else without it.

Disciple: Sir, I can't understand this.

Swamiji: And you needn't. Only get your mind to cling to Him as far as you can. For then only the great magic of this world will break of itself. But then, you must persevere.[66]

Even if one perseveres and apprehends God, does one comprehend Him or Her? Both Job and Vivekananda may have apprehended God or Goddess but did they comprehend His or Her ways? Is that which is not comprehended to be attributed to evil, to evil deeds or to the evil one or evil ones?

> If Hinduism tends to resolve the disparity between the divine and the human more in terms of the human through karma, and Christianity in terms of mystery, Islam tends to resolve it in favor of God's sovereignty: "God's command is itself the defining feature of right, and what God wills can never be morally impugned. The great medieval theologian Abū Hāmid al-Ghazālī (d. 1111) affirms that 'there is no analogy between his justice and the justice of creatures. . . . He never encounters any right in another besides himself so that his dealing with it might be a doing of any wrong.'"[67] However,

> This emphasis on God's omnipotence does not mean that Muslims (any more than Calvinists) view God as a capricious despot. On the contrary, their constant affirmation is that God is "merciful and compassionate." Yet in the encounter with suffering, man's response must not be to complain, to question, or even to try to defend God. Hence, for Islamic orthodoxy at least, theodicy remains an undeveloped dimension of the religious life. Its place is taken by the sentiment conveyed by the Qur'anic formula "Hasbuna Allah" ("God is sufficient unto us").[68]

XII

I was still not satisfied. Was there any other avenue left to explore? With considerable reluctance I began to contemplate consulting a guru. The reluctance sprang from the fact that it seemed like a compromise with self-reliance; the temptation arose from the fact that in matters of truth one must be source-blind. In the popular Hindu text, the *Yoga-Vasistha*, Vasistha, the preceptor, tells Rama, "The reasonable words of even a child should be accepted while the preposterous ones should be discarded like straw, even if uttered by Brahmā Himself." I had as yet not heard anything from the mouth of babes, except that Elaine Pagels's daughter liked the idea of her father having being born elsewhere, in answer to her question about where he had gone. And Brahmā had not spoken.

While not consciously searching for a guru, I was, however, conscious of them, though not conscious of their need so far. In fact many leading Hindu or trans-Hindu figures had no guru—Mahatma Gandhi, Aurobindo, Ramana Maharshi—and seemed to get along very well without one. And Krishnamurti had disowned not only guruhood but precocious messiahship, and had denied the need to have a guru, although his followers virtually treated him like one. This had prompted Ninian Smart to remark, during the course of a lunch at the Santa Barbara Airport, that it tells us something about the modern mentality that it needed a guru (i.e., Krishnamurti) to tell us that one did not need a guru. This was also when he alerted me about the forthcoming book by the daughter of Krishnamurti's lover (gulp!).[69]

However, although these people may not have had gurus, and may have furthermore disclaimed the status for themselves as well, was it not just possible that gurus might have privileged access to the workings of the universe denied to me? It was certainly something worth looking into.

Slowly and eerily the realization started dawning on me that the people I might so consult had been dying with alarming rapidity. Mahatma Gandhi, whom one might have consulted, was felled by an assassin's bullet in 1948. I was eight years old, and the only theodicy I needed then was an explanation of why my father or mother slapped me when they did! I do recall the occasion of Mahatma Gandhi's death. Our mother assembled the children in the dining hall, told us about this holy man who had been killed, and asked us to pray for the peace of his soul. It is one of the few sincere prayers I have ever said in my life; the rest were soon to become tainted by self-serving desires. It was easy to pray sincerely when you didn't know who God was and who Gandhi was. Now one knows who Gandhi was, but God?

The next person who began making an impression on me as someone who might know the score was Ramana Maharshi. You guessed it, he went in 1950, though he denied that he was "going anywhere." "Where can I go?" he is believed to have remonstrated to his followers when they implored him not to leave them.

Then in 1986, during a visit to Oxford, I met Freda Wint. She was the wife of Guy Wint, a British journalist whose work had impressed me for two reasons: his criticism of British imperialism and his observation that the USSR was also an imperialist country, a realization obscured by the fact that its territorial expansion occurred gradually on the contiguous Asian landmass and went virtually unnoticed, while other European countries were busy acquiring colonies overseas in a more dramatic manner. The full significance of his observation has only now become apparent with the dissolution of the USSR. But I digress.

Freda Wint surprised me with a copy of Nisargadatta Maharaj's *I Am That*[70] with the beguiling inscription, "In memory of a beautiful evening, full of cognitive dissonance and other interesting events." It was handed to me as I checked out of Linton Lodge to head home, which was then Australia. The book made a strong-enough impression on me that I inquired whether the person whose words it recorded was still alive! You guessed it—he had died in 1983. I was crestfallen but not despondent—the gap was closing. The difference in years between my wanting to see a "guru" and his "leaving the body" was narrowing. In the case of Nisargadatta Maharaj, I even got a consolation prize: I met someone in Sydney who had seen him in the flesh. Although he had virtually called her names at times, she didn't seem to mind! In fact Lydia told us that his last words to her, as she bowed to take leave of him, were "*You* are the eternal truth." Soon the swami himself died of cancer, moaning, we are told, the name of a beautiful Thai disciple who had been ordered out of his hovel (he was a bidi maker) by his family because her robes were too diaphanous—transparent like the truths the Master himself taught.

They were gone, but their writings were with us. I rummaged through them for that pearl—nay, diamond—of great price with which I could cut open the glass ceiling of the limits of theodicy I had run into in each religion. Gandhi had said, in order to know why

God allows evil, you have to be God! Ramana Maharshi, when the same question was put to him, had once said, more enigmatically, "Who is asking the question?" And Nisargadatta Maharaj had said something less enigmatic but still profound: "You suffer with what you identify." So even if I did not get full satisfaction I was not about to claim a refund.

And then it happened in the mysterious way these things are supposed to happen. A "living Master," a "realized soul," had just arrived in, where else, California, and was staying in (where else?) Los Angeles in a palatial mansion near Beverly Hills. I flew down from Montreal to meet him. It was an experience worth writing home about, but as I am not in touch with my family I wrote it up for posterity (who else?), although posterity hasn't written anything for me yet, nor is it likely to. That long story must be cut short, cut to the bone—the broken bone of my leg. Here was the Master to whom I could put the question, and to earn bonus points I put it to him in Sanskrit: why did I break my leg?

"My brother died this morning," was the answer I got.

His statement had a strange effect on me. It brought about a sudden shift in my consciousness, as if someone had suddenly changed the TV channel. It was as if he were saying, Grow up. My brother just passed away and you are hung up about your stupid knee you may have broken several years ago. In other words, he was telling me what the black girl at the counter told me in America when I asked her if I could pay my dues in Canadian dollars: "Get real." This guru had Zenned me out!

A few weeks later he died too! Had I been spiritually more precocious, or secularly more suspicious, or had he been younger, I could have wondered about his motive. But he was eighty-four years old. Death is the ultimate non sequitur. My guru had died on me.

XIII

My first serious bid to explain what had overtaken me in the form of having my bone (and also almost my spirit) broken in the prime of my midlife was to seek an explanation in terms of predetermination. It happened because it had to. This had the merit of leaving the issue of who the predetermining agent might be—God, or karma, or some other agency—altogether open. It also had the merit of taking everybody off the hook, not least oneself. If somehow it was predetermined, as Stephanie's dream seemed to hint, then there was no need for tearing one's hair. One could still look for the answer in terms of agency, but one did have an answer of sorts—an interim or proximate answer, while one went after the ultimate one. For a while this seemed to satisfy me, and I reached a point where I could identify with the formulation of the fate-versus-free-will debate as found in Islam, which "maintained the Peterine parallel of the potter and the vessels; Allah could do as he pleased with his own. *The orthodox difficulty was rather man's consciousness of freedom.*"[71] It was with this difficulty I had to contend, not just in terms of everything being decreed by God, as I was willing to accept other options here, but with the fact that if everything *is* predetermined, then how do we have the feeling, even if it be illusory, of possessing free will unless that was also predetermined? This view also seemed to coincide with one understanding of the position of Ramana Maharshi on the point, as elaborated by Arthur Osborne in the following passage (in which Ramana Maharshi is referred to by the honorific "Sri Bhagavan"):

> Sri Bhagavan was uncompromising in his teaching that whatever is to happen will happen, while at the same time he taught that whatever happens is due to *prarabdha*, a man's balance-sheet of destiny acting according to so rigorous a law of cause and effect that even the word "justice" seems too sentimental to express it. He refused ever to be entangled in a discussion on free will and predestination, for such theories, although contradictory on the mental plane, may both reflect aspects of truth. He would say, "find out who it is who is predestined or has free will."
>
> He said explicitly: "All the actions that the body is to perform are already decided upon at the time it comes

into existence: the only freedom you have is whether or not to identify yourself with the body." If one acts a part in a play the whole part is written out beforehand and one acts as faithfully whether one is Caesar who is stabbed or Brutus who stabs, being unaffected by it because one knows one is not that person. In the same way, he who realizes his identity with the deathless Self acts his part on the human stage without fear or anxiety, hope or regret, not being touched by the part played. If one were to ask what reality one has when all one's actions are determined, it would lead only to the question: Who, then, am I? If the ego that thinks it makes decisions is not real and yet I know that I exist, what is the reality of me? This is only a preparatory, mental version of the quest that Sri Bhagavan prescribed, but it is an excellent preparation for the real quest.[72]

I could not, however, hold on to this position for long. For one thing, although Stephanie's dream could doubtless be regarded as precognitive, as Marie Royer, my psychologist friend, pointed out, such dreams may indicate possible future paths rather than the certainty of that being the only one. Dreams may represent possible actualities rather than actual certainties. This was the most persuasive nondeterministic interpretation of the precognitive dream that had been offered to me. Further exploration of Islam also revealed at least two other modes of reconciling God's will with a human being's: that while *ontologically* everything depended on God, *morally* human beings were responsible. In a sense this was a replay of the karma argument by analogy—that although everything is drawn to the center of the earth, this fact does not prevent one from ascending a staircase, even though in the process of performing that act too one is continuously being drawn to the center of the earth. Or that whether one runs or falls, or whether one wins the race or loses it, *all* these actions involve the operation of gravity. The second attempt at a reconciliation was by *theoretically* regarding everything as literally happening according to the will of God, but *practically* acting as if one were responsible. But even Islam, with its well-known emphasis on God's will, rejects *jabr*, or absolute determinism.[73] This also resonated with the view of karma that only *after* every possible effort in the present has been exhausted may the occurrence of an event be ascribed to inevitable past karma.

The question of the source of predetermination could also not be kept in cold storage forever. The question "Man can do what he wills, but can He will what He wills?" now turned into the question "God can do what He wills, but can He will what He wills" given the *karma* of the creatures?[74] And as for *karma*, the fact that it is beginningless could imply, or worse, conceal, an infinite regress.[75]

The controversy over predetermination and free will, as it were, ran its predetermined course freely! Ramana has said about the issue of fate and free will, "The answer to this question, if given, will be rather difficult to understand. Yet almost everyone asks this question some time or other in his life."[76] I had asked this *question* as an *answer* to my question: why the accident? But that question did not seem to possess a final answer. So I was forced to return to my original question: how are predetermination and free will to be reconciled? I turned to Islam again, which has long grappled with the issue *without* the intervening variable of karma, and was told,

> It is evident that the doctrine of divine unity implies predestination. Where God is and naught beside Him, there can be no other agent than He, no act but His. "Thou didst not throw, when thou threwest, but God threw" (Koran 8.17). Compulsion is felt only by those who do not love. To know God is to love Him; and the gnostic may answer, like the dervish who was asked how he fared:
>
>> "I fare as one by whose majestic will
>> The world revolves, floods rise and rivers flow,
>> Stars in their courses move; yea, death and life
>> Hang on his nod and fly to the ends of earth,
>> His ministers of mourning or of joy."

This is the Truth; but for the benefit of *such as cannot bear it*, Jalaluddin vindicates the justice of God by asserting that men have the power to choose how they will act, although their freedom is subordinate to the divine will.[77]

I was among those who could not "bear it" and was too committed to karma to allow for the subordination of my will to God's. In this context I may be said to possess what the British whimsically refer to as the "American virtue of insubordination."

XIV

Suffering, in some cultures, has been viewed as the gateway to God through which the lame would walk. I tried, but I stumbled. Suffering did not add to the meaning of life for me; if anything it subtracted from it. However, I could not overlook a belief of my own tradition that him whom God favors he deprives of everything, presumably so that one is left with God alone. In fact, in the famous epic the *Mahabharata*, the heroine Draupadi asks God to keep her in suffering that she may not forget him.[78] A bit perverse, I thought. One could also remember him by gratitude—the memory of the heart. Nor can I overlook the evidence of the Christian tradition in which Christ's vicarious suffering is said to have brought about human beings' at-one-ment with God by a massive transfer of terrible karma. However, we were not here dealing with mystical suffering in which one suffers the death of one's "self," or martial suffering that calls forth heroism. The pain I had to deal with was the pedestrian pain of being hit by a car while walking, as if my own karma had backed into me! Moreover, despite my disinclination to accept such a conclusion, even in such suffering people *had* found meaning. Joseph Campbell told Bill Moyers,

> I had an illuminating experience from a woman who had been in severe physical pain for years, from an affliction that had stricken her in her youth. She had been raised

a believing Christian and so thought this had been God's punishment of her for something she had done or not done at that time. She was in spiritual as well as physical pain. I told her that if she wanted release, she should affirm and not deny her suffering was her life, and that through it she had become a noble creature that she now was. And while I was saying all this, I was thinking, "Who am I to talk like this to a person in real pain, when I've never had anything more than a toothache?" But in this conversation, in affirming her suffering as the shaper and teacher of her life, she experienced a conversion—right there. I have kept in touch with her since—that was years and years ago—and she is indeed a transformed woman.[79]

I would like to distinguish this sensational example from a widely prevalent view. There is a hoary philosophy that perhaps human beings can learn only through suffering. I could never bring myself to accept this point of view and my accident did nothing to convince me that my belief was erroneous. If anything, suffering can learn a lot from human beings, the way many of them bear it. Even if this heroic attempt at a somersault of sensibilities is not entirely convincing and some find the theatrical element in it a trifle nauseating, I hope the point has been made. Even if people seem to grow through suffering, they may do so despite it.

I think a whole generation must be inoculated against the idea that suffering is a necessary schoolmaster. Deepak Chopra writes about a patient, Barbara, who on being diagnosed having terminal cancer retorted, " 'Well, if I am a terminal case, so are you doctor and so is everyone around me.' He was shocked but as I saw it, if he lived thirty or forty years longer than me, that made no real difference. Dying is inevitable; it is a natural part of life, and what I had realized, what gave me such peace of mind, was that dying can be an adventure."[80] I have, however, to agree with Deepak Chopra, who describes this case as follows:

> Despite Barbara's sense of jubilant conversion, I have to insist that something has gone awry here. Disease is no way to solve the core issues of life. We are weakest when sick, least able to summon the resources that are needed for real transformation. The beauty of Barbara's conversion does not automatically cancel the suffering that went with it. Nor does it settle the crucial issue of whether suffering was needed in the first place. An age-old belief says that suffering is inevitable, deeply human, and even a grace. Barbara felt that she had learnt from her pain, and took pride in that. "I'd rather live six months with this cancer," she told me at one point, "than seventy years the way I was." However, without taking anything from the bravery of her response one cannot overlook the fact that under the circumstances, she had little other choice than to feel this way; the alternative was to be crushed by the forces set against her. But whatever meaning people feel can be derived from their personal suffering, to live without pain would, I believe, be even more meaningful, even more human. People have to be transformed *before* the crisis. If not, they may find themselves with not enough time to enjoy the life that suddenly seems so worthwhile.[81]

I couldn't help wondering, however, whether there was a connection between life and language that psychology had as yet not disclosed to us. My friends tell me that I am driven (when I tell them I don't drive!). Did I literally need a break? Was that all the accident was about? Is life just a rhetorical flourish? Did I, through my accident em-brace (my leg was put in a brace) a new way of life, or a new woman in my life? (Where is she?) However, the possibilities may not be infinite here, in fact they may amount to India's contribution to the world: zero, for all that I just suggested could be a literalist fallacy masquerading as pop psychology.

XV

My broken leg had quickened my search for a theodicy to a degree and to an extent that I was myself slow to realize. Initially I was rather nonchalant about it, as if a tentative belief in predetermination combined with willed determination as I went about my physiotherapeutic exercises would soon put me past my present condition. When the arc of recovery did not curve as gracefully as I had hoped, I was compelled to consider the matter more philosophically rather than just medically. However, I was still lackadaisical about it, as a natural worldview seemed enough to calm my philosophical disquiet. But as the days progressed and it became clearer that the prognosis was less certain than I had imagined, doubts began to corrode my confidence and I started gravitating toward a rational worldview that my accident after all did have an apparent cause—my stepping off the sidewalk in front of a car. It was an ambulatory version of the husband being the last to know! What could be more apparent? I could not, however, rest satisfied with that apparent explanation for long, any more than one can rest satisfied with a symptom and not look for the cause, once one stopped confusing the two.

This upped the ante and lifted me on the plane of the moral worldview, and that is where I stayed for quite a while, wondering about my bad karma. However, the buck did not stop there, for while some schools of Hindu and Indian thought dispense with God once karma has been enthroned as an explanation,[82] the more orthodox view considers God as the dispenser of karma.[83] Moreover, the law of karma is itself regarded as an expression of God's will in theistic Hinduism,[84] so that finally I too had come face to face with the trilemma that characterizes traditional Christian theodicy. The problem of theodicy

> arises when the experienced reality of suffering is juxtaposed with two sets of beliefs traditionally associated with ethical monotheism. One is the belief that God is absolutely good and compassionate. The other is the belief that he controls all events in history, that he is both

all-powerful (omnipotent) and all-knowing (omniscient). When combined with some other explicit beliefs—for example, the belief that a good being would try to prevent suffering insofar as he is able—these various ideas seem contradictory. They appear to form a logical "trilemma" in the sense that, while any two of these sets of ideas can be accepted, the addition of the third renders the whole logically inconsistent.[85]

The silver lining to the proverbial dark cloud, however, did not fail to shimmer. A few months before I had been felled, my colleague Gregory Baum had been confined to bed by a viral infection of the inner ear, which had completely immobilized him for eight weeks. He had to lie in utter darkness during this period, and on his recovery he delivered a short sermon in the chapel at McGill University on his illness. The moment I came to know of this I grabbed hold of it and devoured it in one sitting.

The three horns of the trilemma had gored him no less than me, for he began his sermon by confessing that he found the traditional Christian notion of unconditional surrender to the will of God, "what Jesus had done in the garden," very difficult to accept. This was compounded by the fact that if "according to traditional theology, Jewish and Christian, God does not will evil directly; still, God permits it to happen," then after such troubling events of the twentieth century as the Holocaust and Hiroshima, Gregory Baum was forced to ask himself, "Can one surrender oneself to God, if this divinity has allowed the new darkness of the twentieth century?"

Gregory Baum offered new theological variations of the old themes. In terms of God's will, he then "dropped the question whether my illness was God's will. God's will, I felt, was my healing—'spiritually understood.' God does not will sickness; on the contrary, God is the principle of life, the source of the spiritual and physical energies that enable people to transcend their wounded condition and live richly and deeply." Although Gregory Baum did not say so, he seemed to imply this not just of God but of the trinitarian God as well. He referred to Jesus as the healer (*Christus medicus*), and the healing activity of the Holy Spirit is too well known to require comment.

One of the standard theological answers to the trilemma is the free-will theodicy—that God allows evil to occur notwithstanding his omnipotence, for otherwise the creatures' exercise of free will seems to have little meaning. This point has come under theological fire recently,[86] but if we choose to operate within the terra firma of received wisdom in the field, as Gregory Baum did, two points of view become significant. Gregory Baum wrote that he "strongly felt . . . during the first two weeks when I was in constant misery" that "if this condition were to be chronic, the gracious God, life-giver and rescuer, would allow me to put an end to my life. This went against the teaching of the church. Still, in my misery I received great consolation from the idea that God had *left me this last door to freedom.*"[87] The free-will theodicy normally does not take *such* an exercise of free will into account in Christian circles. I could, however, easily relate to this concept of self-willed death, and not confuse it with suicide in light of my Indian background.[88] Gregory Baum also felt that the concept of "God's omnipotence must be understood differently. Omnipotence refers rather to God's limitless power to create, to redeem, to heal, to reconcile and restore." In Hinduism, the presence of a God like Shiva, who is a destroyer and yet a God, already predisposes one to such an interpretation, for among other things the omnipotent God of destruction can also destroy destruction.

I considered myself very fortunate and uniquely privileged in having access to the theological and philosophical resources provided by Professor Gregory Baum. The Chinese have a saying: "Same bed. Different dreams." Now we had a new version of it: "Same suffering. Different theodicies!" And yet, were they that different? They may have been different, but there was no sense of difference. When the search for meaning intensifies, the distinctions among religions and philosophies tend to blur and even vanish. The fact that both of us underwent our physical trials more or less simultaneously provided occasion not only for mutual commiseration but for ecumenical discussion. In fact, in his sermon, Professor Baum was able to breathe life into such apparently arid Aristotelian concepts as those of Pure Act and Unmoved Mover when applied to God:

Here we have then the two technical terms: God as Pure Act and Unmoved Mover. What do these terms mean? If they are not clarified with the help of the hylomorphic theory, they sound abstract and heartless, as if the divinity, perfect in heavenly splendour, were unmoved by the fate of men and women.

When the Scholastics called God Pure Act, they suggested that God was not a being, that God differed from all beings inasmuch as God was fully realized and activated, free of all potency. For example, God was fully loving: God's love could not increase, because God was love. And secondly—this is important in our context—God was related to men and women not so much as heavenly ruler but as the creative, life-giving, actualizing presence at the core of their being. God was mover: which was to say God was the gracious, vivifying presence in their lives that enabled them to actualize their potency—to grow, develop, become wise and loving. God was mover, prompting men and women to enter more fully into their humanity. Today we hold that God is mover, empowering people in their struggle for dignity and justice.

Reflecting on God as Pure Act and Unmoved Mover during my illness, I had the strong realization that people who yearn and struggle for their physical and spiritual health do so because they are so moved by God; their entry into actualization is prompted by the loving God who is totally Act. In moving people to enter into their destiny, God—the Scholastics insisted—is "unmoved," i.e., not in need of a prompter or enabler. God's self-communication in creation, redemption and providence takes place out of the infinite resource of God's own actuality.

If this theology is valid, then the surrender to God in prayer is at the same time an affirmation of all the human struggles for health and well-being, spiritually understood struggles—as we have seen—in which God is graciously present to men and women. These struggles include more especially the wrestling of the exploited and oppressed for the conditions of life in keeping with their dignity. If God is Pure Act, then turning to God does not separate us from our own depth nor from other people. Here the prayer of surrender is no longer frightening since it is a surrender to life and rescue, to the life and rescue of all.[89]

Gregory Baum had provided a philosophically rich theodicy that I was able to use in my own way in a Hindu context. For instance, Hindu thought emphasizes that God is both the illness and the medicine, the wound and the healing—not just creative but all activity.[90] It also contains echoes of the idea of the Unmoved Mover.[91] The difference, from a Hindu point of view, lies in the immanent or pantheistic undercurrent of the Hindu view and the transcendent or properly theistic undercurrent of the Christian. Western theology would probably not cut open the idea of the divine on the dissection table of discussion in the same way. But hey, if the cap fits . . .

It was also useful to have one's suffering put in some perspective. What was a broken knee before the diabolically disfigured remains of millions of victims of a Holocaust, or the otherwise evaporated human beings of Hiroshima? What was his darkness of eight weeks, I cannot imagine Gregory Baum not wondering, in the face of "the new darkness" of the twentieth century! All personal theodicies, unless characterized by pure philosophical inquiry or embraced by a larger quest of meaning, must run into the cul-de-sac of narcissism.

XVI

I have taught only two things, the Buddha once declared in one of his epigrammatic utterances: (1) of suffering and (2) the cessation of suffering. Buddha is better known for his proclamation of the Four Noble Truths,[92] those of (1) the existence of suffering, (2) the arising of suffering, (3) the cessation of suffering, and (4) the path leading to the cessation of suffering. The cognoscenti of comparative religion know that the *two* points mentioned earlier offer an even more concise summation of his teaching. In fact, it could even be reduced to just one, the first truth of *dukkha*, or suffering, for had the Buddha not said, "He who sees *dukkha* sees also the arising of *dukkha*, sees also the cessation of *dukkha* and sees also the path leading to the cessation of *dukkha*."[93] The four truths interpenetrated so thoroughly that the Buddha had even declared that to grasp one of them was to grasp all of them,[94] just as the taste of the entire ocean may be found in a single drop of water.

So why had I fought shy of engaging Buddhism on this point for so long, when even as a fourteen-year-old student I had not shied away from snatching a leaf—as a verboten memento—from the transplanted Bodhi tree at Anuradhapura in Sri Lanka (then called Ceylon) on a school excursion, as a token of my adoration for the Buddha? I had thought the Buddha had dealt with the inescapability of suffering, while I was grappling with the inexplicability of it. We thus seemed to be on different tracks, which may asymptotically ever approach each other, especially in the distance, but could never converge, except in an optical illusion. But soon I began to have second thoughts; what if, in trying to point the way out of suffering, he might have let slip an aside on how we fall into that condition in the first place? True, the Buddha discouraged speculation on origination, but he did encourage the analysis of causation.

My injury was an example of "exposed or evident *dukkha*,"[95] which formed only a minor element in the context of that term, which is "used in a very complex sense impregnated with deep philosophical and psychological nuances, to denote an anguishing, tormenting mental experience of varying intensity."[96] After I had overcome the embarrassment of the superficial nature of my own suffering, it soon became clear to me that my accident was not the *cause* of my suffering; rather, the whole incident was a *symptom*[97] of the human condition in which physical suffering was inevitable by the very nature of things. This is an important point, as it oscillates between a natural and moral worldview. I could have broken my bone because of negative past karma, or I could have broken it just because I got struck by a car, existentially rather than karmically. And only a Buddha could really tell the difference![98]

However, but for the fact of my possessing a body, the accident could not have occurred, hence the natural took precedence over the moral, as it were, for the fabric of being was a necessary presupposition for both, and more fundamental.

Nevertheless, in either case, the explanation of suffering was mental. The term *dukkha* in this sense is "taken to be physical pain which consequently causes mental anguish,"[99] for "mental involvement is a necessary ingredient of *dukkha*. . . . It is not mere sensory experience which causes *dukkha*, but the mental reaction to it."[100] Buddhism distinguishes between pain and suffering—it is the superimposition of the ego on pain that causes suffering. For instance, suppose I had been a football player. How much *more* would I have suffered mentally, as a result of breaking my knee, compared to what I did as a member of a sedentary profession, although the amount of physical *pain* I felt would have been the *same*?[101] From this it follows that the person without an ego will experience pain but not suffering, precisely the claim made about enlightened beings in Buddhism. When the great eleventh-century Tibetan Buddhist mystic Milarepa was dying, he was asked if he did not feel pain, as his agony was so obviously great. "No!" he replied, "But there is pain." There is pain but somehow it is not his.[102] The situation with us mere mortals is very different: "The perceptual process starts on a very impersonal note and proceeds so till the arising of feeling (*vedanā*). With the arising of feeling the process switches over to a personal note making it appear a subject-object relationship, with feeling as an experience of the subject. This marks the intrusion, which to the worlding is no intrusion at all, of ego-consciousness into the field of sense perception."[103] It is this intrusion that converts pain into suffering, *a* toothache into *my* toothache; we all possess body and mind but this sense of "I" the Buddhists regard as something gratuitous over and above and around body and mind, "like the smell of a flower, which is neither the smell of the petals or the pollen but of the flower."[104] So Buddhism had told me *how*, it hadn't still told me *why*.

Buddhism, however, did help one probe the issue further in two directions and although one was broader and one narrower than my specific concern, both were yet relevant to it.

One feature of my accident, perhaps of all accidents, was its suddenness, that sense of loss of control. Buddhism associates this "accident ambience" with the phenomenon of life itself, which the Buddha describes at one point as "just like a mountain river, flowing far and swift, taking every thing along with it; there is no moment, no instant, when it stops flowing, but it goes on flowing, continuing. So . . . is human life, like a mountain river."[105] This gave me the sense as if what I had experienced was an "accident"; it was a subaccident within a larger experience of the accident called life. My question is, if the two accidents represent two concentric circles, one large and one small, do the centers coincide, or was the car accident a small circle on the periphery of the larger?

Perhaps I was imaging the situation in too static a manner. For the striking feature of the accident was not merely that it suddenly happened; it was an equally striking feature of it that it was suddenly over. Was there some lesson to be learnt here in terms of the transitoriness of things? This point is made much of in Buddhist thought:

> Strictly speaking, the duration of the life of a living being is exceedingly brief, lasting only while a thought lasts. Just as a chariot-wheel in rolling rolls only at one point of the tyre and in resting rests only on one point; exactly in the same way, the life of a living being lasts only for the period of one thought. As soon as that thought has ceased the being is said to have ceased. As it has been said: "The being of a past moment of thought has lived, but does not live, nor will it live. The being of a future moment of thought will live, but has not lived, nor does it live. The being of the present moment of thought does live, but has not lived, nor will it live."[106]

The Buddhists describe human personality as consisting of five categories of feelings, volitions, etc., which are described as aggregates and are ever in a state of flux. If pushed to its logical conclusion, this leads to the view that human beings are constantly changing:

> They do not remain the same for two consecutive moments. Every moment they are born and they die. "When the Aggregates arise, decay and die, O bhikkhu, every moment you are born, decay and die." Thus, even now during this life time, every moment we are born and die, but we continue. If we can understand that in this life we can continue without a permanent, unchanging substance like Self or Soul, why can't we understand that those forces themselves can continue without a Self or a Soul behind them after the non-functioning of the body?[107]

I was not interested in pursuing the Buddhist argument for its implications for rebirth because Buddhist psychology is quite alive to the relativity of terms such as "birth" and "death." According to the Buddhists, "birth and death take place simultaneously every moment; and mystics like Milarepa made no difference between this and the other lives—regarding them all as one. 'Accustomed as I've been to meditating on this life and the future life as one, I have forgotten the dread of birth and death.'"[108]

This was one aspect of the accident: not that we experience an accident in a life; life itself can be experienced as a series of accidents, linked or connected accidents. Perhaps life gives the appearance of motion but is a series of stills played out in quick succession, each still the equivalent of an "accident." A sudden stopping of the projection through an "accident" might reveal the truth about these successively darting "accidents." That did not happen to me, although early Buddhist literature as well as Zen literature is replete with accounts of how a minor "accident" triggered the onset of Realization. Sometimes, "Salvation is found in the ordinary things of life. Hsuan-Chien was enlightened when his teacher blew out a candle, another when a brick dropped down, another *when his leg got broken.*"¹⁰⁹ My leg was broken, but I had not become enlightened.

My narrower interest focused on the fact that the Buddha has once sustained an injury to his leg as a result of a stone thrown at him by the envious cousin Devadatta. This incident raised not only eyebrows but questions. If the Buddha was free from any taint of evil karma, how could this happen? Moreover, how could anyone even do this to someone as great as him? Such questions surface in the purported dialogue between the Greek king Menander (whose name is Sanskritized as Milinda) and the Buddhist monk Nagasena, in a text assigned to the first century CE known as *Milinda's Questions*. The answers shed a flood of light on the questions preoccupying us. The incident we are dealing with may first be described in fuller detail: "During many hundreds of thousands of births, sire, Devadatta has borne malice against the Lord. Because of that malice he released a great rocky stone, the size of a gabled house, and thought: 'I will make it fall on the Lord.' Then two rocks rose up from the earth and crushed that rocky stone (though) a fragment, on being broken off from it by (the force of) their combined blow, fell in such a way that it fell on the Lord's foot."¹¹⁰

So the incident raised two issues: Buddha's karma, and Buddha's invulnerability. The Buddhist savant Nagasena resolved the issues in the following manner.

On the issue of karma he denied that *all* events are the result of karma as a general principle,¹¹¹ and he further denied that any evil karma on the part of the Buddha was involved.¹¹² Evil karma was involved, but of Buddha's cousin, not the Buddha. As Nagasena explained, "Moreover, sire, that fragment that fell on the Lord's foot (brought as its karmic result) an experiencing of anguish by the ungrateful selfish Devadatta."¹¹³

The Buddha was considered invulnerable in the sense that the earth is said to have paid him homage. Hence the question, why did the earth allow the splinter to fall on Buddha's foot?¹¹⁴ Nagasena responds by saying that "the Lord's foot was grazed by a splinter. But that splinter did not fall down of its own essential law, it fell down owing to Devadatta's treachery."[115] The implication seems to be that the earth would have been moved to protect the Buddha if the splinter had fallen of its own essential nature. As to the further question, why did the splinter not pay respect to the Buddha like the earth? Nagasena provides a list of twelve conditions in which such respect is not paid, but they all relate to people. The point seems to be that it is not the splinter that did not show respect, but Devadatta.[116]

The point of immense interest here is the admission of genuine unpredictability as to where the splinter might fall. In one case, for instance, there is this statement:

> But that fragment, on being broken off from the rocky stone by (the force of) the combined blow (of the rocks), fell *in an unpredictable direction in such a way that it fell on the Lord's foot*. As, sire, fine, minute, infinitesimal dust, when struck by the violence of a wind, falls in an unpredictable direction here and there, even so, sire, that fragment, on being broken off from the rocky stone by (the force of) the combined blow (of the rocks), fell in *an unpredictable direction in such a way that it fell on the Lord's foot*. But if, sire, that fragment had not been detached from the rocky stone, then when those rocks rose up they would have taken hold of that fragment of the rocky stone also. But that fragment, sire, was poised neither on the earth nor in the sky, so that when it was broken off from the rocky stone by the strength of the combined blow (of the rocks), *it fell in an unpredictable direction in such a way that it fell on the Lord's foot*. Or as, sire, sere leaves on being caught by a gust of wind fall in an unpredictable direction here and there, even so, sire, this fragment, on being broken off from the rocky stone by the strength of the combined blow (of the rocks), *fell in an unpredictable direction in such a way that it fell on the Lord's foot*.[117]

So the Buddhist savant was quite prepared to let the chips fall where they may.

THE AFTERMATH: THE SEARCH FOR MEANING / 97

In the same context, elsewhere, the savant allowed that some things could also slip through the net, as it were. When asked why the two rocks that crushed the rocky stone could not crush the splinter as well, he replied,

> As to that, sire, some part of what is crushed (always) *escapes, slips through and gets lost*. As, sire, water taken into the hand escapes through the interstices between the fingers, *slips through and gets lost*, as milk, buttermilk, honey, ghee, oil, the juice of fish, the juice of meat when taken into the hand (each) escapes through the interstices between the fingers, *slips through and gets lost*, even so, sire, a fragment on being broken off from the rocky stone by (the force of) the combined blow of the two rocks coming together for the purpose of crushing it, fell in such a way that it fell on the Lord's foot. Or as, sire, sand that is fine, minute, infinitesimal as dust if taken into the fist escapes through the interstices between the fingers, *slips through and gets lost*. . . . Or as, sire, when a ball of food is taken into the mouth, part getting clear away from the mouth *escapes, slips out and gets lost*, even so, sire, a fragment, on being broken off from the rocky stone by (the force of) the combined blow of the two rocks coming together for the purpose of crushing it, fell in such a way that it fell on the Lord's foot.[118]

Not only does the savant concede the possibility of unpredictability of outcome and allow for a margin of slippage in process as well, he makes a third concession: of the possibility of an accident occurring a priori. For after explaining that what is experienced arises from "eight causes": "originating in the winds (of the body), . . . in the bile . . . in phlegm . . . resulting from a union of the humours of the body . . . from a change of season . . . from the stress of circumstances . . . [arising] suddenly . . . born of the maturing of kamma,"[119] the savant ascribes the splinter incident to something "arising suddenly." He says,

98 / AN ACCIDENTAL THEODICY

> But, sire, when the Lord's foot was grazed by a splinter, what he experienced originated neither in the winds (of the body) nor in bile nor in phlegm, nor was there a union of the humours of the body, nor was it due to a change of season, nor to the stress of circumstances, nor to the maturing of kamma. *It was merely sudden.* For Devadatta, sire, bore malice against the Tathāgata during many hundreds of thousands of births. Because of that malice, he took a great heavy stone and thinking: "I will let it fall on his head," released it. But two other rocks, coming together, crushed that stone before it reached the Tathāgata, though a fragment, broken off by the (force of the) blow, fell at the Lord's feet and drew blood.[120]

One feature of this discussion is even more significant. Nagasena states clearly that "small is what is born of the maturing of kamma, greater is the remainder."[121] *This can only mean that the natural factors possess far more explanatory force than karma in accounting for why things happen the way they do.*

In other words, if all this is brought to bear on my accident then it was just that: an accident was an accident was an accident. But there is a catch. Although it was an accident *for the Buddha*, it was a karmic act *for his cousin* Devadatta. And I am not the "Enlightened one," I am not even enlightened! But this inquiry does raise an intriguing possibility: Could the accident have been an accident for *me* but the karma of the *driver*? Or vice versa? If I run into you, whose karma is it: yours or mine? Buddha's case had suggested that it needn't always belong to both.

XVII

R. C. Zaehner, one time Spalding Professor of Eastern Religions and Ethics at Oxford, is said to have been a Jew who converted to Roman Catholicism. However, one of his last articles to appear in print before he apparently died on the way to the church, bore the title "Why Not

Islam?" He felt, writing at the peak, or may I say, in the heat of the Cold War, that Eastern religions were too wishy-washy to withstand the ideological force of communism—only the prophetic religions had what it takes, and perhaps Islam as *the* prophetic religion was the one to look for, if not turn to, in this crisis. Of course, with the USSR having dissolved into over a dozen independent republics, the issue has been relegated to history. But it suddenly occurred to me, in my groping for meaning: "Why not Judaism?" Perhaps the experience of the Holocaust had thrown the problem of theodicy in that tradition into such bold relief that it had called forth an answer profounder than any I had encountered so far.

We were standing in the foyer of the Faculty of Religious Studies. The year had just a day or two left to it, and it was midafternoon when I suddenly found myself face to face with Professor Baum. We are the two members who most inhabit these halls during vacations. I had just thanked him again for the marvelous meal he and his wife Shirley had treated us to. Professor Baum, I believe, is a former priest and Shirley was a former nun. She has a delightful sense of humor, as I had discovered when, seated next to her at a dinner one day, in response to the hostess's query about how I was doing, I said, "I'm enjoying it so much I must be sinning." And she had quipped: "That is when we are not doing anything!" I had regaled a woman colleague with this remark and added, "It seems former nuns make wonderful wives." "Remember that when you look for one," she had said. It was only later that I recalled that she too had formerly been a nun. Things are no longer simple any more (I almost said single).

They had prepared a special meal—a vegetarian one at that—out of deference to the dietetic scruples of his Hindu and Buddhist colleagues, and the occasion had justified that English expression, "a feast of reason and the flow of soul." And crumbs were still falling from that theological table. I posed my question. He looked somewhat abstractly into the distance momentarily, and said: "Ah, yes. A student of mine did a doctoral dissertation on that, you know. There are several responses from modern Judaism. One view is that the Holocaust poses no special problem."

"It doesn't?" I said with some incredulity, although one gets used to everything in the study of religion.

"No," he affirmed. "According to this view the death of an innocent child qualitatively raises the same question," he continued, shifting his weight to the other foot. The death of an innocent child was an expression freighted with emotion for me. Memories flooded my mind: of Mark, the son of Elaine Pagels, to whom she dedicated the book that she had so kindly autographed; of my own sister, who died of meningitis at the age of nine and, one almost chokes to admit, was probably blind during her final hours, during most of which, mercifully, she was in a coma; and of a teenager, Danny Williams, also from meningitis, in Knowlton.[122] He had asked that soul-searing question, in slurred speech, his body covered in a rash: "Why me?" I paused long enough to steady myself and resumed the conversation.

"It is only a difference of scale then," I said, braiding my arms and firming my feet on the dark green carpet that sliced the hall-space into two neat halves.

"Yes. Then there is the view that the age of 'untroubled theism' is over. Systematic destruction of life on such a scale renders belief in God troublesome, though still possible. But there is a dialectic of disbelief built into it. The more you believe that God is love, the more difficult it becomes to believe in God. Some Jews have abandoned faith in God for belief in religion."

As I tried to fathom this beguiling turn of phrase, Professor Baum helped me along by adding, "These Jews admit that belonging to the religion of Judaism is a positive thing, in terms of identity and so on, but it is no longer possible to believe in God."

As I heard this, my mind wandered to India. Is the political revival of Hinduism there to be understood similarly? Can Hindus countenance a God that inflicts the kind of humiliation Hindus have undergone—at least in their perception—at the hands of Muslims, Christians, and now secularists? Or was this an exaggerated, even overblown, parallel? But Professor Baum's next remark broke my reverie and sucked me back into the discussion. The chandelier cast a glow on his face as it swayed to the draught of cold air that came in as someone opened the main door while he said: "And some have said that God suffered with them too."

I perked up. I said: "This is what Susannah Heschel, the daughter of Abraham Joshua Heschel, confirmed to me as her father's interpretation." I found a certain tragic beauty in the idea. God suffering with his people—did not Jesus? But Professor Baum had read my mind.

"In Christianity, Jesus suffers, but not God. I find it hard to grapple with, this idea of God suffering, though I don't quite know why. It has probably something to do with the idea of a perfect being. A perfect being does not suffer."

"Or else a perfect being could suffer perfectly." I said very tentatively, as in the study of theology the extent of my knowledge of that subject has never come close to even matching the extent of my interest in it. Then I continued.

"But is not an impassible God an impossible God," pausing to add, "especially for process theologians."

"I have yet to understand process theology," Professor Baum said modestly. That to me was all right. I have never understood Hinduism. But he went on, largely encouraged I suspect by my ignorance. "They speak of the two poles of God, one that is involved in the world . . . However I think there is a certain consolation to be derived from the transcendence of God. The wicked can make the righteous suffer, but God is within the reach of the righteous alone, who are devoted to God, unlike the wicked. This is a source of strength." "Like a nest egg, secure from the daily fluctuations of our financial fortunes," I added, fearing that I was giving too much away about the current state of my financial affairs.

He began to laugh at the analogy but good humouredly agreed. "The idea of suffering with 'com-passion' is a mystical one . . ." I ventured gingerly.

"Yes, it is not biblical in the accepted sense," he added, but did not slam the door shut on that possibility.

Did God break a leg too when mine broke?

Stephanie insists, however, that after the Holocaust the terms of the debate over theodicy have been radically altered, as Elie Wiesel maintains. Will I get a chance to hear him in Boston?

Judaism also offered a new angle on the distinctions I had drawn between moral, rational, and natural theodicies, by suggesting a ritualistic interposition that partook of all three. The natural worldview poses the least problem in terms of explaining suffering; a ritualistic worldview, I now discovered, comes next in terms of offering a simple explanation. The ritual worldview, however, must be carefully distinguished from the moral worldview, with which it can be often confused. A couple who suddenly lost their nineteen-year-old daughter attributed this loss to not having fasted on Yom Kippur.[123] A teenager, however, attributed the fact that he was diagnosed as shortsighted to the fact that a few days before, he had "spent several minutes looking at the pictures of unclothed women" in *Playboy* and thought that now, "God had begun the process of punishing him with blindness for looking at those pictures."[124] The teenager was functioning with a moral worldview, the parents of the girl with a ritual worldview. Often it takes a comparative religionist to disentangle these elements in the worldview of a particular religion. For instance, the first four of the Ten Commandments are particularistic and ritualistic; the last six are moral and universal.

The Holocaust relates the problem of theodicy to the first four of the Ten Commandments, or more particularly to the first, but what of those who kept not only those four but also the other six? Modern Judaism has faced the question of theodicy not just in its most egregious manifestation in the Holocaust, but has also addressed, by comparison, the more quotidian expressions of that problem, as when Harold S. Kushner tries to explain why bad things happen to good people. The problem is that most if not all of us look on ourselves as good people, or at least as good people whose lives have somehow gone wrong because of a traumatic experience while young—now beyond recall! So where are the bad people? The issue then becomes: when bad things happen to people; if the title of his book *When Bad Things Happen to Good People* had been *When Bad Things Happen to People*, would all the "good" people have still bought it in such large numbers? In any case, could my broken leg really be placed on par with a crushed bone, and a fracture be explained in the same breath as the genocide of six million Jews? For once I was in principle prepared to be a Marxist and to maintain that a change in quantity led, after a point, to a change in quality, that as the quantity of heat applied to water went past a certain point and it changed from a liquid to a gas, its subsequent behavior required an explanation of *a different order*. The explanation of my broken leg may well have to qualitatively differ from that of the Holocaust—one could not place them on the same footing. With a broken leg one couldn't do that anyway.

XVIII

I had drawn up the threefold scheme of moral, rational, and natural worldviews independent of any specific religion or philosophy, and they may therefore be designated as commonsensical. The classification pertained to the degree to which "theodicy," understood in its broadest sense as the need to explain suffering, arose in relation to these worldviews. How did they differ? According to a natural worldview, rain fell on the saint and the sinner alike. According to a rational worldview, the person who made the channel to his plot gets the water from the channel and not the others, although it is the same rain that falls on the saint and sinner alike that fills the dam. According to the moral worldview, God wipes the world out in a deluge but spares Noah and his kin. Then there was the upper cone consisting of the theistic, monistic, and nondualistic worldviews, which could in various ways be connected with the moral, rational, and natural worldviews of the lower cone. The vast ground that was then traversed by me in search of an actual theodicy led to many intellectual adventures, and I now faced the following question: in my search for a theodicy satisfying to me, was I to ignore this journey and start from point zero, or was I going to draw on the material I had encountered as possible resources for this theodicy?

The answer often depends on who is asking the question. Was I asking this question as a pristine monad or as someone already possessing a cultural self, which may have shaped the question in its own way notwithstanding the universality of the problem of suffering? All human beings possess noses, but all noses are not the same. It was then my cultural nose that the accident had put out of joint. It was as a cultural self—as one belonging to the Hindu world horizontally and the academic world vertically—that I was asking the question, standing quizzically at their intersection.

Everyone belongs to a religion and culture, but no one accepts all of one's religion or culture. Which ideas and ideals of my background, Hindu and academic, did I accept and feel free to use as building blocks for my "theodicy"? The answer soon became clear: ideas of karma, rebirth, and God I clearly and uninhibitedly accepted from my Hindu background, and it was out of these—as enriched by the comparative study of religion—that a theodicy had to be fashioned that would satisfy me. Perhaps it was inevitable that I should go back to my roots: "The accent of one's birthplace persists in the mind and heart as much as in speech."[125]

In the second chapter of his Gospel, St. Luke refers to a man called Simeon as seeking "the consolation of Israel." My concern was more narrow. I was seeking my own consolation. Each of the levels—the moral, the rational, the natural—not to speak of the theistic, the monistic, and the nondualistic, or a combination thereof, was capable of providing it. I broke my leg. Ramakrishna had broken his arm: "The body is really impermanent. When my arm was broken I said to the Mother, 'Mother, it hurts me very much.' At once She revealed to me a carriage and its driver. Here and there a few screws were loose. The carriage moved as the driver directed it. It had no power of its own. Why then do I take care of the body? It is to enjoy God, to sing His name and glories, and to go about visiting His jnanis and bhaktas."[126]

I could not, however, experience such emotional comfort. What the Goddess had provided Ramakrishna with was not an answer; it was only the allegorization of his question, although that seemed to do for him as an answer, leading one to the Ingersollian reflection that "an honest God"—or Goddess—is the noblest work of man. That raises a profound question. Despite Gandhi's suggestion that to know why evil exists in God's world, one must be God, one must now wonder whether God himself knows the answer. Or perhaps the question does not fit God's case, just as the question "what is the colour of air" does not fit the case. Could it be that there is no point in seeking a divine answer to a human question: a human question can only have a human answer, if any? After all, "What a piece of work is man! . . . In apprehension how like a God," even if a "ruined God," according to Emerson.[127]

This view lies at the core of the idea that evil in relation to God is not evil, it is so only in relation to man, even if we overlook the complication that its concept may not merely be human but also vary from one human being to another. The idea finds a place in Hindu, Islamic, and Judaic theisms, and I dare say in others as well. For Ramakrishna (1836–1886), evil was no more evil for God than poison is poison for a snake; Jalaluddin Rumi "does in a sense make God the author of evil, but at the same time he makes evil intrinsically good in relation to God—for it is a reflection of certain divine attributes which in themselves are absolutely good. So far as evil is really evil, it springs from not-being. The poet assigns a different value to this term in its relation to God and in its relation to Man."[128] Martin Buber's articulation is more theologically freighted, but mines the same vein: "The so-called evil is fully and as a primary element included in the power of God, who 'forms the light and creates darkness' (Isaiah 45:7).The divine sway is not answered by anything that is evil in itself, but by the individual human beings, through whom alone the so-called evil, the directionless power, can become real evil."[129] One could interpose here the question: does the Confucian view claim that the Will of Heaven holds empires rather than individuals under its sway?

However, the relationship of God to evil seems to be capable of reformulation, as the formulation of the concept of God itself is moved from a personal to an impersonal dimension. In fact, a different metaphor can illustrate each of these stages, each stage representing an attenuation of the identification of "goodness" with God. In the most personal formulation, God is all good, God is all light; evil hangs around his hem like darkness on the outer perimeters of light. At worst one might even regard evil as the human shadow of divine light—a darkness that cannot exist unless a shadow is cast by it, when it is obstructed by human perversity. If God is viewed in both personal and impersonal terms, then it is still possible to connect God with goodness and light on the basis of God's love being something personal, but his wrath could be impersonal, as Professor Dodd has demonstrated.[130] Impersonal reality, however, in relation to good and evil, "transcends both and at the same time explains them. To cite an illustration which is as old as the Upanishads: It is like the sun which explains the phenomena of day and night, but at the same time transcends them in that it knows no night, nor even day in our sense of the term."[131] Therefore if the ultimate reality or Godhead is impersonal it is also neutral, in terms of opposites. The same electricity that cools the refrigerator heats the radiator. This last example no doubt changes the metaphor from that of light to heat, though one hopes that it generates the former.

The doctrine of karma doubtless offered some rational comfort:

> If every man could interfere with the events of the world at his own will and pleasure, what a chaotic world it would be! No, no. The law of karma, far from filling us with despair, fills us with hope. It teaches us that, in the moral world as well as in the material world, nothing happens by chance. Just as a savage, who dreads a storm or an eclipse as a sign of the anger of his gods, ceases to dread it when he comes to know the laws of nature, so when we come to know the law of karma, we cease to dread the arbitrariness of chance, *accident* and luck. In a lawless universe our efforts would be futile. But in a realm of law, we feel secure and guide ourselves with the help of our knowledge. When we know that sin entails suffering, that we shall reap as we sow, and that our entire future will not be decided by what we do or fail to do in a single life time, but that we shall be given as many chances to improve ourselves as we want, we are filled with hope. When we know that we are the architects of

our own fortunes and that it is never too late to mend, we feel strong and secure. We are glad that we are not at the mercy of a capricious God.[132]

Even if I took the word *accident* here literally and personally I could not track it down to the specific past karma that might have caused it. My memory began to fade the further I moved into the past, and my earliest recollection stopped at being carried on the shoulders of an attendant at a height from which I could peep just over the hedge, to get a glimpse of the Ganges River as it flows through Banaras. Nevertheless, it is true that sometimes karma would seem like a satisfying explanation—but only sometimes. At other times I would wonder, like Rajchandra, Gandhi's quasi-guru, that if I had suffered for my bad karma or sin and "people suffered from their own sins . . . what drove them to sin?"[133] In other words, self-pity and compassion for others sometimes seem to burst the banks of karma. "In the logical mind of Rajchandra, there was not a single hurt, a single cry of pain, which could not be prevented if men were compassionate enough. But there was a price to be paid for these victories: a man of true compassion would inevitably suffer unendurable torment"[134]—like Gandhi?

Then there was Ramana and his relentless insistence on not so much individual responsibility as the responsibility of individuality in the matter of suffering. A profound insight is involved here. The question of justice always involves an individual or individualized unit. Justice is always personal—individual (not divisible) in this sense. In the impersonal dimension, justice is a nonissue. For Ramana it was *more* than due to karma—it was rooted in radical ignorance, which produces individual existence of which karma is just an aspect. He refused to hold creation responsible. He said,

> Creation is neither good nor bad; it is as it is. It is the human mind which puts all sorts of constructions on it, seeing things from its own angle and interpreting them to suit its own interests. A woman is just a woman,

> but one mind calls her "mother," another "sister," and still another "aunt" and so on. Men love women, hate snakes, and are indifferent to the grass and stones by the roadside. These value-judgments are the cause of all the misery in the world. Creation is like a peepul tree: birds come to eat its fruit, or take shelter under its branches, men cool themselves in its shade, but some may hang themselves on it. Yet the tree continues to lead its quiet life, unconcerned with and unaware of all the uses it is put to. It is the human mind that creates its own difficulties and then cries for help. Is God so partial as to give peace to one person and sorrow to another? In creation there is room for everything, but man refuses to see the good, the healthy and the beautiful. Instead, he goes on whining, like the hungry man who sits beside the tasty dish and who, instead of stretching out his hand to satisfy his hunger, goes on lamenting, "Whose fault is it, God's or man's?"[135]

It is evident from the last line that he refused to hold God responsible either. As he elaborated elsewhere:

> Whose karma is it? There are two creations, one God's and the other man's. The former is single and free from karma. The latter is varied and has varied karmas. If man removes his own creation, there will be no varied individuals and no varied karmas; misery will thus disappear. He who kills man's creation sees heaven only, the others see only hell.[136]

XIX

Matter may not matter, but how did one overcome the mind? Never mind? Could these key concepts accomplish together what they could not do for me singly? No such solution synergized for me. I made

THE AFTERMATH: THE SEARCH FOR MEANING / 109

my prostration to Ramana and kept going on my own road. That road led not to a temple but to a theater.

Aesthetic theodicy is not unprecedented; I live under the illusion that mine might be!

We all know how Shiva "dances the cosmos into and out of existence,"[137] and can one get more aesthetic than this?

> Ramakrishna used to see a long white thread proceeding out of himself. At the end would be a mass of light. This mass would open, and within it he would see the Mother with a Vina. Then She would begin to play; and as She played, he would see the music turning into birds and animals and worlds and arrange themselves. Then She would stop playing and they would all disappear. The light would grow less and less distinct till it was just a luminous mass, the string would grow shorter and shorter, and the whole would be absorbed into himself again.[138]

However, the aesthetic theodicy I have in mind is based on certain philosophical presuppositions. The first is that to look for justice in the universe is to look for the wrong thing at the wrong place at the wrong time, such as an accident. It is like looking for the watch where there is light and not where it was lost. It is at the time of an accident, a death, or a setback, that we ask about justice: why don't we ask about it in the course of daily living? True, Newton also, according to the story, discovered the law of gravitation when the apple hit him on the head. But he did not curse the blow, he discovered the *law* of gravitation through an *incident* of it. That law, however, explains why buildings stand as well as why they fall. Is the law of gravitation just? To look for justice is to look for the wrong thing. To look for justice is to look at the effect rather than the cause; moreover, it is looking at the effect from our point of view. One must, therefore, disabuse one's mind of values, of looking at things as they should be, and first look at things as they are.

This leads to the second presupposition: that it is our presuppositions in light of which we assess the outcome and its theodicean problematic. Two examples must suffice. If we start with an idyllic condition, an Eden, then there is the problem of the fall and a sense of loss. If, however, we start out with a fallen state, even a little positive development is a great gain. Thus Augustine would cry because we fell from heaven, but if we rose even a little toward heaven from a woe-begotten world, Irenaeas would weep for joy. If life is presumably meant to stand for happiness, then anything that goes wrong has gone horribly wrong. If life is presumably meant to stand for suffering, then even a little happiness goes a long way. Hence, not only must we dispense with the idea that there must be a steady state of justice in a dynamic world, we must dispense with the idea of a given starting point.

Now the third point. The various theodicies surveyed can all be reduced to two basic types: what might be called *cosmos* theodicies and what might be called *chaos* theodicies; alternatively, they could be called *frugal* theodicies or *extravagant* theodicies. How is this distinction to be explained? If I get hit by a car in summer in Montreal when car traffic *increases* and my accident is explained in terms of such increase, which also increases the probability of an accident, then here we have the example of an *extravagant* theodicy. If, however, my accident is explained as my being at the wrong place at the wrong time, regardless of the amount of traffic, because I was destined to be hit, then the same accident serves as an example of a *frugal* theodicy. It will be tempting for students of Hinduism to label the former a *lila* theodicy and the latter a *karma* theodicy. It would be tempting, but it would also be misleading, if both the concepts are simultaneously accepted, for then God could be visualized as juggling *karmas* in his *lila* as the cosmic magician. If the two concepts are kept apart from each other, a case could be made for their congruence with the earlier analogy, but typically they are *not* kept apart. God is *karmādhyakṣa*,[139] the supervisor of karma: "Individual human beings have to suffer their karmas for His purpose. God manipulates the fruits of karma; he does not add or take away from it. The subconsciousness of man is a warehouse of good and bad karma. Iswara chooses from this warehouse what He sees will best suit the spiritual evolution at the time of each man, whether pleasant or painful. Thus there is nothing arbitrary."[140] It is as if to celebrate this fact that dances have conventional forms and even games are played according to certain rules. In the theodicy I am going to develop, I intend to separate them without severing them.

> One final point. Indian thinkers have maintained that none of the Indian systems is finally pessimistic; and the common view that they are mostly "gospels of woe" is entirely wrong. We have more than one interesting indication in the Sanskrit language of this faith of the Indians in the ultimate goodness and rationality of the world. The Sanskrit word *sat*, as noticed long ago by Max Mueller, means not only "real" but also "good." Similarly the word *bhavya*, we may add, means not only "what will happen in the future" but also "what is auspicious," implying that the best is yet to be. Corresponding to this belief on the practical side, there is the belief on the theoretical side that ignorance or error will also be superseded in the end by truth for which, as one old Buddhistic verse puts it, "the human mind has a natural partiality." If either evil or error were final, the world would be irrational.[141]

The last sentence is the most significant. In one way it makes eminent sense; looked at another way, it still makes sense but in a very different way. That it makes eminent sense is suggested by the following example. When we say that law and order prevails in a city such as Montreal (it is wise to select a Canadian rather than an American city in this context), does it mean that thefts are not committed in Montreal? Of course thefts are committed in Montreal. So when we say that law and order prevails in Montreal what it means (apart from the fact that the incidence of crime might be low) is that *when* thefts are committed the *thieves* are ultimately apprehended and brought to book.

However, how long is ultimate? One month? Six months? One year? In fact there can be no fixed ultimate, for different kinds of crimes are being committed and criminals are being apprehended all the time, but for different crimes. One might say that in an individual case the case is closed when the guilty party is caught, but by the time that happens the government may have denied the *same* person whose stolen car was recovered a proper tax refund for which he must now seek redress. In other words, there is no ultimate or final outcome—justice viewed comprehensively *is a process, not an outcome.*

The worldview I propose, then, is essentially Hindu in that it has no beginning and no end, and it has a God. And God arranges events, sometimes in consequence of a person's karma and sometimes just for dramatic effect, or *lila*. However, if for dramatic effect and no other reason God pauperizes the virtuous, then God can always, like life is an unending soap opera, suddenly make the same person win the lottery, again for dramatic effect. However, these dramatic effects are karmically commensurate from the point of view of God the dramatist, just as the other events of a person's life may be karmically commensurate from the point of view of his or her own karma. Thus there is a two-track karma in operation here—that of God and that of the beings. God can always, at some future date, reorder events in the interests of justice, as a novelist in a later part of a novel might redeem one unjustly condemned in an earlier part. This then is the meaning of suffering—it thickens the plot, either on account of your own past dramatic karma or God's. Sometimes life may also lack much drama—novels can be dull for some stretches. Now: if God can act out of character—so to say, nonkarmically—perhaps so can a human being. A human being might buck the current karmic trend on a whim, but his or her arbitrary action does not mean, any more than God's, that that person will not be karmically rationalized in the long run in which we are not only dead but reborn. Thus, although one may act initially in a nonkarmic way, the action can ultimately never remain nonkarmic, although the ultimate could be a long way away.

Life is an interplay of God's and human beings' acting out their *lila* and karma. God is not merely a judge, he is also a dramatist. Life is not a trial in a city court, but more like television's

Nightcourt—God also plays Matlock and Perry Mason, not just the judge. And so do we.

It seems that the ancient seers of India entertained both the possibilities—the cosmic theodicies as well as the chaos theodicies—for they have their roots ultimately in cosmology. In one famous metaphor, the universe is said to emerge from and be withdrawn in the ultimate reality the way a spider spins out the web and withdraws it within itself. This resonates with the cosmos theodicy. In another famous metaphor, the universe is said to emerge from it as countless hairs crop up on the head, or as grass grows on the earth. This resonates with the chaos theodicy. All that I have done is to place the spider in the splendor of the grass.

XX

I had reached this point in my exposition when I had to interrupt my sabbatical at Boston and return to Montreal for a few days. My colleague, Katherine Young, and I finally located an open restaurant on Mackay Street and trumpeted our success to her husband, Tom, across the street. Tom also teaches at McGill—meteorology, one winces as one writes, given the snowstorm we had run into.

"So have you discovered the meaning of life in Boston?" Katherine asked, once we had thawed out with the help of liberal draughts of the necessary liquids. "No more in Boston in the US of A than in Montreal of Canada and Sydney of Australia," I replied, citing earlier abodes. "I must admit though that the chance was least in Sydney." "Why?" She looked surprised.

"Haven't you heard? They say that while the rest of the world asks: what is the meaning of life, Sydneysiders ask: where can I find waterfront property?"

Katherine, who had been to Sydney, laughed before commenting: "But you are no closer to it in Cambridge. You have to pierce the Chares River mystique first even to get to the problem."

Ah. The problem. But I did figure out the problem.

"I finally figured out why I feel uneasy with life," I said. "It is like being made to participate in a game when you are unacquainted with its rules. We are forced to live without knowing or being told the rules of the game of life."

I have never been taken so completely by surprise as I was by Katherine's comment when she said, "I thought you knew the rules rather well." The yawning chasm in our perceptions of the situation astonished me, and I found myself gaping at it.

I was still struggling with the cognitive dissonance generated by Katherine's comment when Tom chirped in. "Are there any rules? Or isn't it rather that we make them as we go along?"

As I took in Tom's remark, I had the sinking feeling that I was back to square one. As if it were part of a psychic defense mechanism, however, I found my mind drifting away. I was having a flashback!

A young lad of thirteen had just joined the Modern School in New Delhi, now that his parents had moved to New Delhi from Lucknow. It was sports hour prior to the classes and he stood bemused at the boundary of the soccer field, not knowing what to do with himself as all his classmates rushed on to the field and began to play. Soon the imposing figure of a physical instructor approached him. "What are you doing standing out there?" he demanded to know.

"This is my first day at school."

"So?"

"I don't know how to play soccer."

"You don't?" The figure, embodying muscle as well as authority, had moved closer to the lad by now.

"No."

"There is only one way of knowing how to play. By playing." The comment was accompanied by a firm movement of his hand, which propelled the lad onto the field. To this day the lad doesn't know whether it was a pat or a push. Perhaps a bit of both.

As the boy stumbled onto the field, he shouted, "But what are the rules of the game?"

He could barely hear the instructor's response, for they were being drowned out by the commotion in the field: "That too you learn as you play."Soon he saw a football approach him with four boys pursuing it, and then the ball was at his feet and he had no choice but to start playing.

NOTES

PART I

1. Could it be that I had internalized the following worldview, even more than I dare to acknowledge to myself, in the course of my Hindu upbringing? According to one perspective,

> None can ever be the cause of fortune or misfortune of another. The *karman* which we have ourselves accumulated in the past, that alone is the cause of fortune and misfortune. To attribute one's fortune and misfortune to another is an error, as it is a vain pride to think: "It is I who am the author of this," for all beings are bound by the chain of their *karman*. If man fancies to himself that some beings are his friends, others his enemies or are indifferent to him, it is according to the *karman* that he has worked out himself. It is necessary, therefore, that man should bear with one mind his fortune and misfortune, which are only fruits of his own action. (Louis Renou, ed., *Hinduism* [New York: George Braziller, 1962], 197)

2. An extreme example of this edifying attitude, even without the underpinning of karma, is provided by the following Hindu myth:

> The sage Bhrigu once desired to know who was the highest god. He devised a test in his mind and decided to administer it to all the strong candidates. First he approached Brahma, the creator god, who also happened to be his father. He sat down in front of Brahma without offering the customary respect.

Brahma could not tolerate such careless flouting of manners and reprimanded him very angrily. The sage then went to Shiva, the god of deconstruction, and began heaping verbal abuse on him without any provocation. Shiva threatened to kill him with his famed trident. Bhrigu ran for his life. The sage subjected to his test other candidates like Indra among the gods and Durga among the goddesses. No one passed the test.

Bhrigu went to the milky ocean to test Vishnu, the god of sustenance, who lies there on the bed of Shesha, a coiled cobra. On being told that Vishnu was incarnating as Krishna on the earth, the sage went to Dvaraka where Krishna used to live. Krishna was asleep in his bedroom. Bhrigu forcibly entered the bedroom and, getting up on the bed, kicked Krishna hard on the chest. As Krishna got up on his rude awakening, he joined his palms, greeted the sage, and apologized for not being ready to offer hospitality due to a guest, especially such a renowned sage as Bhrigu. He even started to massage Bhrigu's foot, saying his hard chest might have hurt the sage's tender foot.

Overwhelmed by his humility, love, and respectfulness, the sage declared Krishna, an incarnation of Vishnu, to be the highest god. Krishna politely accepted the award and said that he would wear the mark of Bhrigu's foot on his chest for ever. The traditional pictures of Vishnu and Krishna still exhibit Bhrigu's footprint as a mark of humility, affection, and accessibility characteristic of one so powerful as not to need any such qualities. (Ramesh N. Patel, *Philosophy of the Gita* [New York: Peter Lang, 1991], 1)

3. F. S. Growse, trans., *The Ramayana of Tulasi Dasa*, ed. R. C. Prasad (Delhi: Motilal Banarsidass, 1978), 324, doha 170.

4. See Tal Brooke, *Sai Baba: Lord of the Air* (New Delhi: Vikas Publishing House Pvt. Ltd., 1979); Vinayak Krishna Gokak, *Bhagvan Sri Sathya Sai Baba: An Introduction* (New Delhi: Abhinav Publications, 1975).

5. The context was provided by the statement, "Destiny is the storehouse out of which all this manifestation flows. It is the principle out of which you have emanated. It is something like the negative of a film; consciousness is already present in that source from which you have emanated, so the film is being projected. What is to be projected is already recorded; so whatever activities happen through that beingness—which is you—are your destiny.

Every action, every step which that beingness will take is already registered in the film." In this quotation, Q stands for the Questioner, or seeker, and *M* stands for the Master.

> Q: . . . The negative exists before the destiny starts. Where is the negative printed?
>
> M: That is the skill of Mula-Maya [primary illusion].
>
> Q: Do all the efforts that we make in this regard have any effect in destroying the sense of "I Am," or is that part of the film? So the effort that people think they are making to reach the goal has no effect, it is just all contained in that film?
>
> M: Be in that source which is the light behind consciousness. You are not the consciousness, understand that. What is happening is in that Mula-Maya.
>
> The cassette records what I am saying, but whatever is recorded in the cassette is not me. Just as the original voice is not in the cassette, so you are separate from the chemical, the body, the "I Amness," the consciousness.
>
> Q: Is the realization in the film?
>
> M: It cannot be in the film because you are the knower of the film. Now ponder whatever you have heard and come back at five o'clock. . . . [pp. 140–41]
>
> Q: Yesterday Maharaj spoke of the chakras [centers of psychic energy in the body], and the Brahma-randhra. I wondered if we should be concerned with them in our meditation.
>
> M: Forget about chakras. Catch hold of the knowledge "I Am" and become one with it; this is meditation.
>
> Q: Who is to catch hold of the "I Am"?
>
> M: Who is asking this question?

Q: Are we able to go beyond our thoughts, or, in the Absolute, are the thoughts just part of the film, and if they are, do we just have to bear with them?

M: Who wants to go beyond thought? Who is he? Before consciousness appears in the waking state, that is the Absolute; as soon as the consciousness appears the thoughts come. You do not have to bear with them, nor discard them; simply know them.

Q: All the other things that determine who you call the original—those things do not exist?

M: But that is only when you reach that original stage, when you are a Jnani.

Q: We are already that.

M: If you knew it there would be no questions, and you would not be here [pp. 141–42]

(See Jean Dunn, ed., *Seeds of Consciousness: The Wisdom of Sri Nisargadatta Maharaj* [New York: Grove Press, 1982], 139–42.)
6. Ibid.
7. Wilfred Cantwell Smith, *Islam in Modern History* (Princeton, NJ: Princeton University Press, 1957): 109.

PART II

1. This is not as trivial a comment as it sounds and in fact is typical of the Islamic attitude as epitomized in the statement: *bila kaifa* (Without asking why; that is, without questioning God).
2. Edward C. Dimock, Jr., and Pratul Chandra Gupta, trans., *The Maharashtra Purana* (Honolulu: East-West Center Press, 1965), xv.
3. Or, viewed from another point of view,

Laws of nature do not make exceptions for nice people. A bullet has no conscience; neither does a malignant tumor or an automobile gone out of control. That is why good people get sick or get hurt as much as anyone.

The point can be elaborated further:

> Laws of nature treat everyone alike. They do not make exceptions for good people or for useful people. If a man enters a house where someone has a contagious disease, he runs the risk of catching that disease. It makes no difference why he is in the house. He may be a doctor or a burglar; disease germs cannot tell the difference. If Lee Harvey Oswald fires a bullet at President John Kennedy, laws of nature take over from the moment the bullet is fired. Neither the course of the bullet nor the seriousness of the wound will be affected by questions of whether or not President Kennedy is a good person, or whether the world would be better off with him alive or dead.

(See Harold S. Kushner, *When Bad Things Happen to Good People* [New York: Avon Books, 1981], 58.)

4. Ibid., 47.
5. Ibid., 52.
6. Ibid.
7. Ibid., 54.
8. Ibid.

9. That later Buddhism clearly allowed for the operation of natural causes is apparent from the following comment of Deng Ming-Dao in *The Seven Bamboo Tablets of the Cloudy Satchel*: "Nature and her animals are innocent. We may think nature cruel and unmerciful when we find a deer's carcass or see a tree torn by a thunderstorm. This is nature's way and nature's logic. She lacks the wishful thinking and stupid sentimentality that humans possess." Cited in Gerald Tomlinson, ed., *Treasury of Religious Quotations* (Englewood Cliffs, NJ: Prentice Hall, 1991), 170.

10. M. Hiriyanna, *The Essentials of Hindu Philosophy* (London: George Allen & Unwin, 1949), 57.

11. "The Lord who has chosen this cavity of the lotus of the heart for his habitation and shines there as 'I' is one who is worshipped at 'guhesa' (the cave dweller). If the idea that you are this 'guhesa' becomes through practise as firm in your mind as the idea is now firm in it that you are the body and you become that God, the ignorance which identifies you with this perishable body will vanish like darkness before the sun." See A. Devaraja Mudaliar, ed., *Gems from Bhagavan* (Tiruvannamalai, India: Sri Ramanasramam, 1985), 33.

12. D. S. Sarma, *Hinduism through the Ages* (Bombay: Bharatiya Vidya Bhavan, 1956), 138.

13.

Q: We see pain in the world. A man is hungry. It is a physical reality, and as such, it is very real to him. Are we to call it a dream and remain unmoved by his pain?

A: From the point of view of *jnana* or the reality, the pain you speak of is certainly a dream, as is the world of which the pain is an infinitesimal part. In the dream also you yourself feel hunger. You see others suffering hunger. You feed yourself and, moved by pity, feed the others that you find suffering from hunger. So long as the dream lasts, all those hunger pains are quite as real as you now think the pain you see in the world to be. It is only when you wake up that you discover that the pain in the dream was unreal. You might have eaten to the full and gone to sleep. You dream that you work hard and long in the hot sun all day, are tired and hungry and want to eat a lot. Then you get up and find your stomach is full and you have not stirred out of your bed. But all this is not to say that while you are in the dream you can act as if the pain you feel there is not real. The hunger in the dream has to be assuaged by the food in the dream. The fellow beings you found so hungry in the dream had to be provided with food in that dream. You can never mix up the two states, the dream and the waking state. Till you reach the state of *jnana* and thus wake out of this *maya*, you must do social service by relieving suffering whenever you see it. But even then you must do it, as we are told, without *ahamkara*, that is without the sense "I am the doer," but feeling, "I am the Lord's tool." Similarly one must not be conceited and think, "I am helping a man below me. He needs help. I am in a position to help. I am superior and he inferior." You must help the man as a means of worshipping God in that man. All such service too is for you the Self, not for anybody else. You are not helping anybody else, but only yourself.

(See David Godman, ed., *The Teachings of Sri Ramana Maharshi* [London: Arkana, 1985], 211–12)

14. D. S. Sarma, *A Primer of Hinduism* (Madras: Sri Ramakrishna Math, 1981), 58.

15. M. Hiriyanna, *Indian Philosophical Studies* (Mysore: Kavyalaya Publishers, 1957), 128-29.
16. Renou, *Hinduism*, 197.
17. *Darshan* 14:59 (May, 1988).
18. But profoundly: "When anything happens, we are prone to attribute the same to something or someone else. However the fact is that our experiences have already been created by ourselves and nothing happens which is more or less than what we deserve. What can others do to us?" And again: "Others are not responsible for what happens to us, they are only instruments of what would happen to us some way or other. Let us be strong in faith and not succumb to fear. Whatever happens happens according to our *prarabdha* (destiny). Let us exhaust it." See Paul Brunton and Munagala Venkataramiah, *Conscious Immortality: Conversations with Ramana Maharshi* (Tiruvannamalai, India: Sri Ramanasramam, 1984), 134. Joseph Campbell testifies to the tremendous impression this attitude of the Tibetan refugees made on him after they fled from Chinese persecution; Joseph Campbell, *The Power of Myth*, ed. Betty Sue Flowers (New York: Doubleday, 1988), 158-59.
19. Cited in Tomlinson, *Treasury*, 230.
20. Hiriyanna, *Essentials*, 55.
21. Tomlinson, *Treasury*, 80.
22. Ibid., 121.
23. Ibid., 56.
24. Ibid., 55.
25. Ibid.
26. Ibid.
27. Ibid.
28. Ibid.
29. Ibid., 191.
30. Henry Ward Beecher, cited in Tomlinson, *Treasury*, 145.
31. Brunton and Venkataramiah, *Conscious Immortality*, 180.
32. Sri Mungala Venkataramiah, *Talks with Sri Ramana Maharshi* (Tiruvannamalai, India: Sri Ramanasramam, 1984), 246.
33. Godman, *Teachings*, 210-11.
34. Ibid., 208.
35. Swami Rajeswarananda, ed., *Erase the Ego* (Bombay: Bharatiya Vidya Bhavan, 1974), 29.
36. T. M. P. Mahadevan, trans., *Who Am I?* (Tiruvannamalai, India: Sri Ramanasramam, 1976), 8.
37. Brunton and Venkataramiah, *Conscious Immortality*, 77.

38. See Mudaliar, *Gems*, 16. At their root is the "I"—thought (ibid.). However, the mind is not a real entity: "There is no entity by the name of mind. Because of the emergence of thoughts, we surmise something from which they start. That we term 'mind'" (Brunton and Venkataramiah, 164). It is possible to misunderstand Ramana's statement about the illusory nature of these things. According to him existence, consciousness, or Brahman is the sole reality and anything viewed *apart* from it becomes illusory. Take, for example, the illusoriness of the world, an idea associated also with the school of Advaita Vedanta, and its foremost propounder, Śaṅkara. Ramana takes pains to point out, "It is not at all correct to say that Advaitins or the Sankara school deny the existence of the world or that they call it unreal. On the other hand it is more real to them than to others. Their world will always exist whereas the world of the other schools will have origin, growth, and decay, and as such cannot be real. Only, they say that the world as world is not real but that the world as Brahman is real. All is Brahman, nothing exists but Brahman, and the world as Brahman is real" (Mudaliar, *Gems*, 8).

39. Godman, *Teachings*, 208.
40. Ibid.
41. Ibid., 208, emphasis mine.
42. Ibid.
43. Ibid., 212.
44. B. V. Narasimha Swami, *Self-Realization: Life and Teachings of Sri Ramana Maharshi* (Tiruvannamalai, India: Sri Ramanasramam, 1968), 100.
45. Ibid., 102.
46. Ibid., 103.
47. This aspect of Ramana Maharshi's conduct mystifies me. When asked whether he felt the sufferings of others he would declare that he would not be *jñānī*—a true person of wisdom—if he did and yet he would often be deeply moved, sometimes to tears, by the suffering of not only human beings but animals. This dimension of his existence is almost as paradoxical the claim that Jesus Christ was fully human and divine at the same time. The following explanation on the paradox has been offered:

> The Maharshi's reaction to the sorrows of Echammal calls to mind his remark that "the jnani weeps with the weeping, laughs with the laughing, plays with the playful, and sings with those who sing, keeping time to the song. His presence is like a pure mirror. It reflects our image exactly as we are. It is we that play the several parts in life. How is the mirror or the stand on

which it is mounted affected? Nothing affects them, as they are a mere support." Like the art of tragedy, the look of the sage transforms pain and makes it impersonal. As with Echammal, so with many others, suffering turned into life-long devotion.

(See K. Swaminathan, *Ramana Maharshi* (New Delhi: National Book Trust, 1975), 25–26.)

It also seems worth asking: Does it not raise a problem for theodicy as to "why such suffering should come to one so good" as Christ, Ramakrishna, and Ramana? Does the suggestion of vicarious atonement for the sins of others on their part suffice as an explanation?

48. Swami Sambuddhananda, *Vedanta through Stories* (Bombay: Ramakrishna Ashram, 1959), 44–45.

49. S. S. Cohen, *Guru Ramana: Memories and Notes* (Tiruvannamalai, India: Sri Ramanasramam, 1974), 99, emphasis mine.

50. Stephen Mitchell, *Tao Te Ching* (New York: Harper & Row, 1988), 106–7, emphasis mine.

51. Huston Smith, *The World's Religions* (San Francisco: Harper, 1991), 216.

52. Reynold A. Nicholson, *The Mystics of Islam* (London: Routledge & Kegan Paul, 1963), 128–29.

53. Burton Watson, trans., *Chuang Tzu: Basic Writings* (New York: Columbia University Press, 1964), 113. The way Chuang Tzu writes about death in general elicits the following comment from A. C. Graham:

> Nothing in Chuang-tzu's unusual sensibility is more striking than the ecstatic, rhapsodic tone in which he writes of death. This does not reflect a disgust with life; like most Chinese thinkers he is neither an optimist nor a pessimist, and thinks of joy and sorrow as alternating and inseparable like day and night or birth and death. Nor is it a matter of treating death as a beautiful abstraction. In "The teacher who is the ultimate ancestor" we read of a dying man dragging himself to a well to look at his disfigured body and wonder what it will turn into, or a sage who lolls carelessly against the doorpost talking to his dying friend after shooing away his weeping family, of others who appal a disciple of Confucius by playing the zither and doing odd jobs by the corpse. In the stories about Chuang-tzu later in the book he goes to sleep pillowed on a skull, is found thumping a pot

(the most vulgar kind of music-making) on the death of his wife, and on his deathbed laughs at his disciples for preferring to have him decently buried and eaten by the worms rather than left in the open to be eaten by the birds. This physical confrontation with death, and mockery of the rites of mourning, for Chinese the most sacred of all, is characteristic of the *Inner Chapters* and of stories about Chuang-tzu himself, but is very rare elsewhere in Taoist literature, even in the rest of *Chuang-tzu*. It is quite without the morbidity of the stress on corruption in the late medieval art of Europe, which reminds us of the horrors of our mortality for the good of our souls. It seems rather that for Chuang-tzu the ultimate test is to be able to look directly at the facts of one's own physical decomposition *without* horror, to accept one's dissolution as part of the universal process of transformation. "The test that one holds fast to the Beginning is the fact that one is not afraid."

(See A. C. Graham, trans., *Chuang-tzu: The Seven Inner Chapters and Other Writings from the Book "Chuang-tzu"* [London: George Allen & Unwin, 1981], 23–24.) This view seems to represent the natural worldview discussed earlier on in this essay.

54. Watson, *Chuang Tzu*, 48–49.
55. *Analects* (14:41).
56.

The morality of Confucianism is closely connected with its view of destiny. A sharp distinction is drawn between heaven and man, the "decree of heaven" and "human action." Whether I am a filial son and loyal minister depends on myself; whether I enjoy riches and long life or suffer poverty and early death is decreed by heaven. Although the decree of heaven is beneficial in the long run (for example, by the removal of degenerate dynasties), it does not necessarily reward or punish the individual. Thus Confucius himself was a sage who, had he become Emperor like Yao and Shun, could have restored good government throughout the world; but by the inscrutable decree of heaven he spent most of his life out of office in a small feudal state. The Confucian does not question that riches and long life are unmixed blessings, but neither does he expect them as a reward for living rightly. He accepts the alternation of good fortune and bad as part of the natural rhythm of things; he does not, like the Buddhist, regard all life as suffering, nor does he, like many Western humanists, support himself by faith in a future Utopia on earth. So long as he fulfils his duty, failure and adversity should not trouble him, since they are due to heaven, not to any fault of his own.

It is interesting to note, however, that Confucius himself did not always live up to this view of destiny. A couple of his sayings suggest a faith that his own mission to restore the way of the sages could not be in vain, that its success was decreed by heaven:

"Heaven gave birth to the moral power within me. What can Huan T'iu do to me?" [Analects, vii. 22]

Since the death of King Wen, has not the responsibility for this culture rested on me? If heaven intended to destroy this culture, later mortals such as I would not have been able to share in it. If heaven is not going to destroy this culture, what can the men of K'uang do to me? [Analects, ix. 5]

But on another occasion when he was in danger we find him rising to a complete acceptance of destiny:

"Whether the Way will be practised depends on destiny; whether the Way will be abandoned depends on destiny. What can Kung-po Liao do against destiny?" [*Analects*, xiv. 38]

(See A. C. Graham, "Confucianism," in *The Concise Encyclopedia of Living Faiths*, ed. R. C. Zaehner [Boston: Beacon Press, 1959], 381.)

57. Swami Vivekananda, *The Collected Works of Swami Vivekananda* (Mayavati Memorial Edition), vol. IX (Calcutta: Advaita Ashrama, 1968), 147.

58. Swami Vivekananda, *Ramakrishna and His Message* (Calcutta: Advaita Ashrama, 1972), 74–76.

59. Ibid. A fascinatingly detailed and enlightening analysis of these events was offered by A. L. Herman at the Fourth International Congress of Vedanta held at Miami University in Oxford, Ohio (April 2–5, 1992) in his paper "Vivekananda and the Theological Problem of Evil."

60. Ronald M. Green, "Theodicy," in *The Encyclopedia of Religion*, ed. Mircea Eliade, vol. 14 (New York: Macmillan Publishing Company, 1987), 435. Rabbi Harold S. Kushner has proposed a remarkably fresh understanding of Job:

Let me suggest that the author of the Book of Job takes the position which neither Job nor his friends take. He believes in God's goodness and Job's goodness, and is prepared to give up his belief in proposition (A): that God is all-powerful. Bad things do happen to good people in this world, but it is not God who wills it. God would like people to get what they deserve in life, but He cannot always arrange it. Forced to choose between a good God who is not totally powerful, or a powerful God who is not totally good, the author of the Book of Job chooses to believe in God's goodness.

The most important lines in the entire book may be the ones spoken by God in the second half of the speech from the whirlwind, chapter 40, verses 9–14:

> Have you an arm like God?
> Can you thunder with a voice like His?
> *You* tread down the wicked where they stand,
> Bury them in the dust together . . .
> Then will I acknowledge that your own right hand
> Can give you victory.

I take these lines to mean "if you think that it is so easy to keep the world straight and true, to keep unfair things from happening to people, *you* try it." God wants the righteous to live peaceful, happy lives, but sometimes even He can't bring that about. It is too difficult even for God to keep cruelty and chaos from claiming their innocent victims. But could man, without God, do it better?

The speech goes on, in chapter 41, to describe God's battle with the sea serpent Leviathan. With great effort, God is able to catch him in a net and pin him with fish hooks, but it is not easy. If the sea serpent is a symbol of chaos and evil, of all the uncontrollable things in the world (as it traditionally is in ancient mythology), the author may be saying there too that even God has a hard time keeping chaos in check and limiting the damage that evil can do. (Kushner, 42–43)

61. Ibid., 79–82.
62. *The Life of Swami Vivekananda by His Eastern and Western Disciples* (Calcutta: Advaita Ashrama, 1979), vol. I, 233.

63. Green, "Theodicy," 435.
64. Vivekananda, *Ramakrishna*, 81.
65. Green, "Theodicy," 435.
66. Vivekananda, *The Complete Works of Swami Vivekananda*, vol. VI, 481–82.
67. Green, "Theodicy," 438.
68. Ibid.
69. Radha Rajagopal Sloss, *Lives in the Shadow with J. Krishnamurti* (Bloomington, IN: Universe, 2011). It has since been published.
70. Maurice Frydman, trans., *I Am That: Conversations with Sri Nisargadatta Maharaj*, Part I (Bombay: Chetana, 1973).
71. H. A. R. Gibb and J. H. Kramers, *Shorter Encyclopedia of Islam* (Leiden: E. J. Brill, 1953), 200.
72. Arthur Osborne, *Ramana Maharshi and the Path of Self-Knowledge* (London: Century, 1987), 42–43.
73. For a detailed discussion see W. Montgomery Watt, *Free Will and Predestination in Early Islam* (London: Luzac & Company, 1948).
74. Sarma, *A Primer of Hinduism*, 55.
75. John H. Hick, *The Philosophy of Religion* (Englewood Cliffs, NJ: Prentice Hall, 1983), 141–42.
76. "Who," *Mahayoga of Bhagavan Sri Ramana* (Tiruvannamalai, India: Sri Ramanasramam, 1984), 191.
77. Nicholson, *Mystics*, 98. Jalaluddin Rumi is referred to as Jalaluddin in this passage. The italics are mine. For an interesting discussion of related points of view see Caesar E. Farah, *Islam: Beliefs and Observances* (New York: Barron's, 1987), 119–24.
78. See Robert Payne, *The Life and Death of Mahatma Gandhi* (New York: E. P. Dutton Co., 1969), 456.
79. Campbell, *The Power of Myth*, 160.
80. Deepak Chopra, *Unconditional Life* (New York: Bantam Books, 1991), 9.
81. Ibid., 10.
82. Hiriyanna, *Essentials*, 61–70. A good illustration of this point is provided by the school of Hindu thought known as Mīmāṁsā, whose followers are called Mīmāṁsakas. A major thinker of this school was Kumārila, usually assigned to the seventh century. On the point that there exists a supreme self called God who possesses such qualities as omniscience, benevolence, etc., "elaborate arguments are adduced by Kumarila to show that there can be no self of the kind, possessing omniscience and such other super excellences. We cannot, for example, satisfactorily account for the presence, it is

said, of misery in a world created by an omnipotent and benevolent God. This difficulty is commonly explained in Indian doctrines by reference to the past karma of living beings; but the Mimamsaka contends that, if karma is thus necessary for a satisfactory explanation of the problems of evil, even after recognizing God, it may well be taken to furnish its full explanation" (Ibid., 134–35).

83. Ibid., 61.
84. Sarma, *A Primer of Hinduism*, 55.
85. Green, "Theodicy," 431.
86. Hick, *The Philosophy of Religion*, 41–42.
87. The italics are mine.
88. See Arvind Sharma and Katherine Young, "The Meaning of *Atmahano Janah* in *Isa Upanisad* 3," *Journal of the American Oriental Society* 110, no. 4 (Oct.–Dec. 1990): 545–602.
89. See Gregory Baum, "Sickness and the Silence of God," *Concilium* 4 (August, 1992).
90. The following parable of Ramakrishna is as relevant as it is entertaining:

> In a certain village there lived a weaver. He was a very pious soul. Everyone trusted him and loved him. He used to sell his goods in the market-place. When a customer asked him the price of a piece of cloth, the weaver would say: "By the will of Rama the price of the yarn is one rupee and the labour four annas; by the will of Rama the profit is two annas. The price of the cloth, by the will of Rama, is one rupee and six annas." Such was the people's faith in the weaver that the customer would at once pay the price and take the cloth. The weaver was a real devotee of God. After finishing his supper in the evening, he would spend long hours in the worship hall meditating on God and chanting His name and glories. Now, late one night the weaver couldn't get to sleep. He was sitting in the worship hall, smoking now and then, when a band of robbers happened to pass that way. They wanted a man to carry their goods and said to the weaver, "Come with us." So saying, they led him off by the hand. After committing a robbery in a house, they put a load of things on the weaver's head, commanding him to carry them. Suddenly the police arrived and the robbers ran

away. But the weaver, with his load, was arrested. He was kept in the lock-up for the night. Next day he was brought before the magistrate for trial. The villagers learnt what had happened and came to court. They said to the magistrate, "Your Honour, this man could never commit a robbery." Thereupon the magistrate asked the weaver to make his statement.

The weaver said: "Your Honour, by the will of Rama I finished my meal at night. Then by the will of Rama I was sitting in the worship hall. It was quite late at night by the will of Rama. By the will of Rama I had been thinking of God and chanting His name and glories, when by the will of Rama a band of robbers passed that way. By the will of Rama they dragged me with them; by the will of Rama they committed a robbery in a house; and by the will of Rama they put a load on my head. Just then, by the will of Rama the police arrived, and by the will of Rama I was arrested. Then by the will of Rama the police kept me in the lock-up for the night, and this morning by the will of Rama I have been brought before Your Honour." The magistrate realized that the weaver was a pious man and ordered his release. On his way home the weaver said to his friends, "By the will of Rama I have been released."

(See Swami Nikhilananda, trans., *The Gospel of Ramakrishna* (New York: Ramakrishna-Vivekananda Center, 1952), 648–49.)

91. The following description of God by Ramana Maharshi seems to fit in well with the concept of the Unmoved Mover:

Without desire, resolve, or effort, the sun rises; and in its mere presence, the sun-stone emits fire, the lotus blooms, water evaporates; people perform their various functions and then rest. Just as in the presence of the magnet the needle moves, it is by virtue of the mere presence of God that the souls governed by the three (cosmic) functions or the fivefold divine activity perform their actions and then rest, in accordance with their respective karmas. God has no resolve; no karma attaches itself to Him. That is like worldly actions not affecting the sun, or like the merits and demerits of the other four elements not affecting all-pervading space. (Mahadevan, *Who Am I?*, 8)

The three cosmic functions are of (1) creation, (2) preservation, and (3) destruction. These plus the acts of bondage and liberation constitute the fivefold activity.

92. Walpola Rahula, *What the Buddha Taught* (New York: Grove Press, 1959), 16–44.

93. Ibid., 27.

94. Ibid.

95. S. K. Nanayakkara, "Dukkha," in *Encyclopedia of Buddhism*, vol. 4, ed. W. G. Weeraratne (Government of Sri Lanka, 1989), 697.

96. Ibid.

97. For the distinction see Lama Anagarika Govinda, *The Psychological Attitude of Early Buddhist Philosophy* (London: Rider & Company, 1961), 72.

98. I. B. Horner, trans., *Milinda's Questions*, vol. 1 (Oxford: Pali Text Society, 1990), 189.

99. Nanayakkara, "Dukkha," 698.

100. Ibid., 699.

101. "It is evident, therefore, that the intensity of *dukkha* on a given occasion is relative to the intensity of the ego-consciousness affecting the relationship between the individual and the object belonging to the world outside" (Ibid.).

102. A. W. Chadwick, *A Sadhu's Reminiscences of Ramana Maharshi* (Tiruvannamalai, India: Sri Ramanasramam, 1966), 20.

103. Nanayakkara, "Dukkha," 700.

104. Rahula, *What the Buddha Taught*, 65.

105. Ibid., 25–26.

106. Buddhaghosa, as cited in Govinda, *Psychological Attitude*, 128.

107. Rahula, *What the Buddha Taught*, 33.

108. Govinda, *Psychological Attitude*, 58.

109. Edward Conze, *Buddhism: Its Essence and Development* (New York: Harper & Brothers, 1951), 203, emphasis added.

110. Horner, *Milinda's Questions*, 255.

111. Ibid., 191–92.

112. Ibid., 191.

113. Ibid., 257.

114. Ibid., 254–55.

115. Ibid., 255.

116. Ibid., 256–57, especially p. 256 n. 7.

117. Ibid., 257, emphasis added.

118. Ibid., 255–56.

119. Ibid.,188. For a detailed discussion of them individually see pp. 188–89, emphasis added.
120. Ibid., 190, emphasis added.
121. Ibid., 189.
122. *The Gazette*, Dec. 29, 1991, A3.
123. Kushner, *Bad Things* (New York: Avon Books, 1975), 8, 10.
124. Ibid., 11–12.
125. This maxim is commonly attributed to François de Larochefoucauld.
126. Nikhilananda, *The Gospel of Sri Ramakrishna*, 397. A *jnani* is a "knower" of God; a *bhakta* a "lover" of God.
127. William Shakespeare, *Hamlet*, in *The Complete Works of Shakespeare*, ed. Wordsworth Edition (Oxford: Shakespeare Head Press, 1996), 2.2.309–13.
128. Nicholson, *The Mystics of Islam*, 97.
129. Tomlinson, *Treasury*, 76.
130. Hick, *The Philosophy of Religion*, 13.
131. Hiriyanna, *Essentials*, 154.
132. Sarma, *A Primer of Hinduism*, 54.
133. M. K. Gandhi, *The Story of My Experiments with Truth*, trans. Mahadev Desai (Washington, DC: Public Affairs Press, 1948), 114–15.
134. Robert Payne, *Mahatma Gandhi*, 125.
135. Godman, *Teachings*, 210.
136. Cohen, *Guru Ramana*, 49.
137. Stella Kramrisch, *Manifestation of Shiva* (Philadelphia: Philadelphia Museum of Art, 1981), xxiii.
138. Vivekananda, *Ramakrishna and His Message*, 112–13.
139. *Svetasvatara Upanisad*, VI.11; also see Sarma, *Primer of Hinduism*, 55.
140. Brunton and Venkataramiah, *Conscious Immortality*, 135.
141. Hiriyanna, *Essentials*, 51.

BIBLIOGRAPHY

Baum, Gregory. "Sickness and the Silence of God." *Concilium* 4 (August 1992).
Brooke, Tal. *Sai Baba: Lord of the Air.* New Delhi: Vikas Publishing House Pvt., 1979.
Brunton, Paul, and Munagala Venkataramiah. *Conscious Immortality: Conversations with Ramana Maharshi.* Tiruvannamalai, India: Sri Ramanasramam, 1984.
Campbell, Joseph. *The Power of Myth*, edited by Betty Sue Flowers. New York: Doubleday, 1988.
Chadwick, A. W. *A Sadhu's Reminiscences of Ramana Maharshi.* Tiruvannamalai, India: Sri Ramanasramam, 1966.
Chopra, Deepak. *Unconditional Life.* New York: Bantam Books, 1991.
Cohen, S. S. *Guru Ramana: Memories and Notes.* Tiruvannamalai, India: Sri Ramanasramam, 1974.
Conze, Edward. *Buddhism: Its Essence and Development.* New York: Harper & Brothers, 1951.
Dimcock, Edward C., Jr., and Pratul Chandra Gupta, trans. *The Maharashtra Purana.* Honolulu: East-West Center Press, 1965.
Dunn, Jean, ed. *Seeds of Consciousness: The Wisdom of Sri Nisargadatta Maharaj.* New York: Grove Press, 1982.
Farah, Caesar E. *Islam: Beliefs and Observances.* New York: Barron's, 1987.
Frydman, Maurice, trans. *I Am That: Conversations with Sri Nisargadatta Maharaj.* Part I. Bombay: Chetana, 1973.
Gandhi, M. K. *The Story of My Experiments with Truth.* Translated by Mahadev Desai. Washington, DC: Public Affairs Press, 1948.
Gibb, H. A. R., and J. H. Kramers. *Shorter Encyclopedia of Islam.* Leiden, Netherlands: E. J. Brill, 1953.
Godman, David, ed. *The Teachings of Sri Ramana Maharshi.* London: Arkana, 1985.

Gokak, Vinayak Krishna. *Bhagvan Sri Sathya Sai Baba: An Introduction.* New Delhi: Abhinav Publications, 1975.

Govinda, Lama Anagarika. *The Psychological Attitude of Early Buddhist Philosophy.* London: Rider & Company, 1961.

Graham, A. C., trans. *Chuang-tzu: The Seven Inner Chapters and Other Writings from the Book Chuang-tzu.* London: George Allen & Unwin, 1981.

———. "Confucianism." In *The Concise Encyclopedia of Living Faiths,* edited by R. C. Zaehner. Boston: Beacon Press, 1959.

Green, Ronald M. "Theodicy." In *The Encyclopedia of Religion.* Vol. 14. Edited by Mircea Eliade. New York: Macmillan, 1987.

Growse, F. S., trans. *The Ramayana of Tulasi Dasa.* Edited by R. C. Prasad. Delhi: Motilal Banarsidass, 1978.

Hick, John H. *The Philosophy of Religion.* Englewood Cliffs, NJ: Prentice Hall, 1983.

Hiriyanna, M. *The Essentials of Hindu Philosophy.* London: George Allen & Unwin, 1949.

———. *Indian Philosophical Studies.* Mysore: Kavyalaya Publishers, 1957.

Horner, I. B. trans. *Milinda's Questions.* Vol. 1. Oxford, UK: Pali Text Society, 1990.

Kramrisch, Stella. *Manifestation of Shiva.* Philadelphia: Philadelphia Museum of Art, 1981.

Kushner, Harold S. *When Bad Things Happen to Good People.* New York: Avon Books, 1981.

The Life of Swami Vivekananda by His Eastern and Western Disciples. Vol. I. Calcutta: Advaita Ashrama, 1979.

Mahadevan, T. M. P. trans. *Who Am I?* Tiruvannamalai, India: Sri Ramanasramam, 1976.

Mitchell, Stephen. *Tao Te Ching.* New York: Harper & Row, 1988.

Mudaliar, A. Devaraja, ed. *Gems from Bhagavan.* Tiruvannamalai, India: Sri Ramanasramam, 1985.

Nanayakkara, S. K. "Dukkha." In *Encyclopedia of Buddhism.* Vol. 4. Edited by W. G. Weeraratne. Government of Sri Lanka, 1989.

Nicholson, Reynold A. *The Mystics of Islam.* London: Routledge & Kegan Paul, 1963.

Nikhilananda, Swami, trans. *The Gospel of Ramakrishna.* New York: Ramakrishna-Vivekananda Center, 1952.

Osborne, Arthur. *Ramana Maharshi and the Path of Self-Knowledge.* London: Century, 1987.

Patel, Ramesh N. *Philosophy of the Gita.* New York: Peter Lang, 1991.

Payne, Robert. *The Life and Death of Mahatma Gandhi*. New York: E. P. Dutton, 1969.

Rahula, Walpola. *What the Buddha Taught*. New York: Grove Press, 1959.

Rajeswarananda, Swami, ed. *Erase the Ego*. Bombay: Bharatiya Vidya Bhavan, 1974.

Renou, Louis, ed. *Hinduism*. New York: George Braziller, 1962.

Sambuddhananda, Swami. *Vedanta Through Stories*. Bombay: Ramakrishna Ashram, 1959.

Sarma, D. S. *Hinduism Through the Ages*. Bombay: Bharatiya Vidya Bhavan, 1956.

———. *A Primer of Hinduism*. Madras: Sri Ramakrishna Math, 1981.

Shakespeare, William. *Hamlet*. In *The Complete Works of Shakespeare*. Wordsworth Edition. Oxford, UK: The Shakespeare Head Press, 1996.

Sharma, Arvind, and Katherine Young. "The Meaning of Atmahano Janah in Isa Upanisad 3." *Journal of the American Oriental Society* 110, no. 4 (Oct.–Dec., 1990): 545–602.

Sloss, Radha Rajgopal. *Lives in the Shadow with J. Krishnamurti*. Bloomington, IN: Universe, 2011.

Smith, Huston. *The World's Religions*. San Francisco: Harper, 1991.

Smith, Wilfred Cantwell. *Islam in Modern History*. Princeton: Princeton University Press, 1957.

Swami, B. V. Narasimha. *Self-Realization: Life and Teachings of Sri Ramana Maharshi*. Tiruvannamalai, India: Sri Ramanasramam, 1968.

Swaminathan, K. *Ramana Maharshi*. New Delhi: National Book Trust, 1975.

Tomlinson, Gerald, ed. *Treasury of Religious Quotations*. Englewood Cliffs, NJ: Prentice Hall, 1991.

Venkataramiah, Sri Mungala. *Talks with Sri Ramana Maharshi*. Tiruvannamalai, India: Sri Ramanasramam, 1984.

Vivekananda, Swami. *The Collected Works of Swami Vivekananda*. Mayavati Memorial Edition. Vol. IX. Calcutta: Advaita Ashrama, 1968.

———. *Ramakrishna and His Message*. Calcutta: Advaita Ashrama, 1972.

Watson, Burton, trans. *Chuang Tzu: Basic Writings*. New York: Columbia University Press, 1964.

Watt, W. Montgomery. *Free Will and Predestination in Early Islam*. London: Luzac & Company, 1948.

"Who?" *Mahayoga of Bhagavan Sri Ramana*. Tiruvannamalai, India: Sri Ramanasramam, 1984.

www.ingramcontent.com/pod-product-compliance
Lightning Source LLC
Chambersburg PA
CBHW031403230426
43670CB00006B/627